BROKEN LIVES, BROKEN MINDS

Broken Lives, Broken Minds

Pamela Roche
with Maggie Allen

for Joss and Michael

I would like to thank

my dear father, who passed away in June 2013, and my
husband, Edward, for all of their support – financial and
otherwise – without which I would not have been able to
fight this case.

My gratitude also goes to my family, my friends and those
professionals who worked tirelessly to help me try to win
this awful thirteen-year battle.

Thank you to Bob and Pamela Hoch of the Rachel
Foundation, for their help and support, their
encouragement and their friendship.

I wish I could thank personally the late Richard Gardner
who pioneered the study of Parental Alienation Syndrome
and who refused to keep quiet about his ideas. PAS has
been written off all too often as a 'junk science' and has
not been properly recognised in the legal system.

Thanks also to my ghost writer, Maggie Allen, for helping
me to write this book, and to The Writing Company
(www.ghostwritingcompany.co.uk) for introducing us.

Editor's notes

Names of people involved in this true account have been changed, with the exception of some well-known professionals, and the given names should therefore be regarded as fictional: any similarity to the names of any persons alive or deceased is purely coincidental.

Where we have shown quotations and excerpts from legal and other professional documents, all typographical, spelling, punctuation and grammatical errors contained within the original documents are printed as such so that the text can be regarded as verbatim.

Foreword

This is one mother's truly shocking story of a heart-wrenching, soul destroying thirteen-year battle against her manipulative ex-husband, against injustice, against courts, against a system that let her down. A system that let her two sons down in the worst possible way.

It begins as an all-too-everyday tale of marriage, children and divorce.

What began with a normal Christmas visit to their father in Albuquerque, New Mexico, back in 1999 has turned into a nightmare filled with expensive lawyers, courtrooms, medical experts whose reports conflict wildly, accusations of the most appalling nature . . . but mainly filled with the pain and anguish of a mother forcibly separated from her two children and seeing those children systematically poisoned against her.

The nightmare's name is Parental Alienation Syndrome, referred to as PAS.

Pam's story . . .

I have so much to tell, finding a sensible starting point is something that keeps escaping me, but I think perhaps a quote from a book written on this same subject by the well-known

American actor, Alec Baldwin, will be as good as any introduction. Mr Baldwin's high-profile divorce battle took him into the awful world of PAS and eventually encouraged him to write about his harrowing experience, just as my own story is unfolding in these pages.

> *"Although my experiences with judges, lawyers, and court-ordered therapists during my own high-conflict divorce proceedings left me outraged over the injustices I believe are endemic to the family law system in our society, I had no desire to revisit them. The pain I suffered, the fear and anger I felt toward nearly all of the principals involved, and the inescapable sense of helplessness and isolation exhausted me . . .*
>
> *Whatever the reasons that an alienating parent gives for their actions, common sense dictates that one need not see a pattern of behaviour listed in a psychiatric manual to understand that this problem is real and destroying the lives of parents and children everywhere . . . PAS is not just a theoretical issue in divorce. It is the issue, and the reason I wrote this book."*
>
> (*A Promise to Ourselves, Alec Baldwin with Mark Tabb*
> © 2008 by Alec Baldwin, published
> by St Martin's Press, NY)

When you are being accused, purposely and vehemently, of something so, so terrible and you are completely innocent, you really need to be able to depend on the people involved who are in positions of trust and authority – people whose knowledge, expertise, and whose judgement can be the difference between you being proved innocent of all charges, or being seen by the whole world to be guilty. You hope that these people, like you, believe in honesty and justice, in full and proper examination of all evidence, all reports, every slightest bit of information that can have an impact on the outcome. You hope that they will make the right decision – the only decision that *can* be right – once they are completely satisfied that all the relevant facts have been put before them in the proper manner.

This is what you hope.

I now know that such a journey through the legal system can go either way – whether you are as innocent as a new-born baby, or guilty as hell – and that your life, the lives of your children and your family, can either be restored to normality or blown apart for all eternity, in a few seconds in time by a judge who, before this awful day, has never met you or anyone involved, and who is simply basing his decisions on what he sees and hears at that time.

Surely, a professional judge, an experienced judge, a *good* judge, knows better than to take everything put before him as true fact? Surely, someone with such power should be familiar with the laws and rulings surrounding the case he is hearing? Surely, a good judge knows when to examine the information he is being fed, and not to blindly take every word without question?

It was indeed a severe lesson to learn that this is not always so.

I had no idea what was going on – never before in my life did I have any inkling that such things could happen – and I knew I needed to find out as much as I could, otherwise how could I even contemplate fighting against something that was obviously so very powerful?

I researched and I read and I took on board as much information as I could find – and this is where I learned about PAS.

The Parental Alienation Syndrome Second Edition – Richard A. Gardner MD: Creative Therapeutics Inc. 1998

Children Held Hostage – Stanley S. Clawar, PhD, CCS, and Brynne V. Rivlin, MSS: American Bar Association 1991

Divorce Casualties – Douglas Darnall, PhD: Taylor Publishing Company, Dallas Texas 1998

They Are My Children Too – Catherine Meyer: Public Affairs, New York 1999

Smoke And Mirrors – Terence W. Campbell: Insight Books Plenum Press, London and New York 1998

Without Conscience – Robert D. Hare, PhD: The Guildford Press, New York and London 1999

A Kidnapped Mind – Pamela Richardson: Dundurn Press, Toronto 2006

Breaking the Ties That Bind – Amy J. L. Baker, PhD: W. W. Norton & Company, New York and London 2007

A Promise to Ourselves – Alec Baldwin: St Martin's Press, New York 2008

Divorce Poison – Dr Richard A. Warshak: Harper Collins Publishing 2002

I am grateful to all of these authors for their work.

'Never think because life has dealt you one dreadful blow that pushes you to the very brink of insanity, that you have had your lifetime's quota.

As long as we are alive, we cannot know what is around the next corner.'

Pamela Roche

June 2013

A supportive letter kindly published with the permission of the author, the leading authority on PAS in the UK...

Dear Ms Roche,

I respond to you in the form of a complement for the book that you have written on the subject of parental alienation which has touched me very much. In fact I could not put the book down until I had completely read it. Your case is typical of so many that I deal with in the courts in the UK, and since you have seen my parental alienation website you will have noted that the chapters of that particular website are part of a book and another book is to be published in due course. It concerns the problems that you have had with not seeing your two lovely sons for so many years and having an opportunity to have a good relationship with them.

It is clear after reading your book that the courts have not been helpful to you in the United States and indeed in the UK. The sad fact is that the children have lost many years of a good mother, having being alienated against her totally unjustly by a vindictive father who will have done a great deal of harm not only to yourself but also to the children.

Your plight as a mother deprived of giving love to your children and they giving you love back is a typical case which should be considered by anyone dealing with family courts. Your book should be passed to judges dealing with cases in the family courts, allegedly providing justice for all concerned.

It occurred to me how much easier it would have been if your former husband had cooperated so that the children would have the benefit of two parents instead of being deprived of one, and only having one parent in their upbringing. I note you quote Hare, a well know psychologist who has dealt with psychopathic personalities. I would very much place anyone who alienates a child against another parent as being psychopathic and the court should have taken note of this and handled the case appropriately.

The International Hague Convention was set up to help people like yourself. The rules are allegedly legal and meaningful but putting them into operation does not always result in a fair case hearing and this continues to deprive loving parents of contact with their children.

I therefore recommend you book most highly and congratulate you on what you have achieved. It will help many other parents and hopefully the Judiciary to make the right decisions in future.

Yours sincerely,
Dr L F Lowenstein,
MA, Dip Psych, PhD

The Hague Convention is law. It exists to ensure that any child or children caught up in their parents' separation or divorce and retained wrongly by one parent, be reinstated in the country where the original custody agreement was made, so that any necessary legal proceedings can be conducted within that jurisdiction, with all essential parties present – the child's doctor, teachers, relatives, friends, neighbours . . . so that the court can get the widest possible overview of the child's situation and be in the best position to determine whether or not that child is, or has been, in any danger from one or other parent. Unfortunately, there are loopholes in the Hague Convention which means this is not necessarily the outcome. That is exactly what happened in this case, as with so many others in today's world of international marriages and easy divorce.

Thirteen years on, one of the boys has severe mental health issues and has been heavily medicated for all of that time. He lives a sort of half-life with his grandmother who is now in her nineties. The other boy is approaching a point where he will not be able to continue living where he is and he cannot support himself financially. *"I was only allowed minimal – and harrowing – supervised visits with my sons. I spent a total of four hours in seven years with them, closely watched by total strangers. I felt like I was the worst kind of criminal – indeed, women in prison are allowed more time with their children than I have had. My eldest boy is now twenty-four."*

This mother still lives in hope that she will have her sons back with her. This is her story. It will shock you. But it is written to help others, hopefully to be aware of the pitfalls and – God willing – to avoid the pain and heartache, the feelings of utter abandonment and hopelessness that this mother has lived with for the past thirteen years.

Chapter one

how my story begins . . .

I am not a writer. I am a mother.
This is not fiction. This is my true story.

It was 1982. I was twenty-one and life was pretty bad, in all honesty. I was very unhappy at home. Having had a very 'normal' upbringing, things changed dramatically when I was seventeen and my mother left to set up home in France, then my father re-married. I found myself living with a stepmother and stepsisters who I really didn't get on with and who excluded me completely . . . Mother and I didn't see each other for four years. I went to work in France for a while as an au pair; I was miserable and would have been the same wherever I had gone. It didn't work out and I came home feeling even more lonely than before. College wasn't working out for me, I had no career and I was emotionally raw from the break-up of my first real relationship: we'd been together for two years and were engaged – he basically dumped me and I was heartbroken. I was desperate to find a better life.

My friends all worked – exciting jobs in the City and the West End. That made it worse, dragging myself through the daytime until they were free to meet up, but feeling out on a limb because they had their careers and everything that went with that. One of my closest girlfriends, knowing I needed a bit of a tonic, suggested we try this new wine bar in South Kensington. It sounded like just the thing and so off we went.

A few drinks and a few laughs later, there he was. John Proctor. The American who wasn't tall and dashing, but he had so much charisma. That elusive quality, that certain something that can draw you in without you realising it – without you knowing how or why it is happening.

So, the charismatic American and I chatted, laughed and enjoyed each other's company. He was older, worldly-wise, confident, easy to be with, attentive and charming. He was interesting to listen to, and he had so much to talk about – he was unlike anyone I had ever known. And he made such an impression on a young, naïve English girl whose life suddenly seemed a whole lot better.

On the nineteenth of August 1983 we were married in Houston, Texas, even though – now looking back from a completely different perspective – I was already seeing warning signs that all was not perhaps as it should be. One thing that really threw me was that John had told me in England that he was divorced, but, once we were in the States, we had to wait weeks for his divorce to come through. It was, I later realised, the first of so many lies. I was a reluctant bride and almost called the whole thing off, but John was always good at persuading me things were fine. For the next two and a half years I embarked on my new life as a young wife in our house in McAllen in the Rio Grande Valley. It was a very odd set-up at home. We lived with John's parents, all together in the one house. I had realised he had a particularly close relationship with his parents, especially his mother. She had had problems trying to conceive and when he was born she treated him as her 'miracle' son – something that carried on even though he was a grown man. It was unnatural, unnerving.

They say you don't know someone until you live with them and that was very true in my case. I had come from a 'normal' middle-class family in Wimbledon, where we lived a very comfortable existence, had family and friends around us and there was nothing particularly out of the ordinary.

I was amazed to discover that my new husband had absolutely no social life, no hobbies or interests – and no friends to speak of, neither in our home area nor from his past in Texas. I never saw him read a book or magazine, he played no sports, wasn't a member of any club or group, didn't drink at all and was really uncomfortable in any social gathering, when he would talk constantly about himself if he did get into a conversation with anyone. His parents were exactly the same – no outside life, just the two of them closely knit with John: they even called themselves 'the Three Musketeers'.

When he wasn't away on business, John spent all of his time either rooted in front of his computer, embroiled in very lengthy and obviously serious telephone conversations (always out of earshot of myself), or in a huddle with his parents 'discussing business'.

'Business' was the family-owned and run company that John's father had set up and John was a director along with the parents. My father-in-law, an agronomist and a strange man whose wife insisted on addressing him as 'Doctor Proctor', even if he was standing right beside her, had developed an organic fertiliser which he later discovered, apparently, was something of a miracle product. It was – so John explained to me – capable of consuming chemical waste, raw sewage and all manner of bio-hazardous materials. It just looked like a fine black powder to me, but I'm no scientist.

More than once I overheard his mother arguing with people on the phone about unpaid bills, including her threatening to sue the landlord of the enormous house we all lived in, because she said he was harassing her when he chased her for the rent money. She didn't seem to grasp that the point was, the rent payments were two months in arrears.

John's credit rating was dreadful. He blamed this, along with his lack of any personal money, on his ex-wife's excessive spending, adding that she had run up massive bills which he had been left to pay off. This was, of course, the reason he gave me as to why his mother handled all of the family finances, wrote all the cheques, and – I can hardly admit this – why I had to go to her to ask for money whenever I needed anything. She completely controlled all of the money in and out of the household and that's just how she liked it – full control.

I noticed quite early on that John's mother had a penchant for the most expensive clothes and cars – she was always changing her car and she dressed only in *haute couture*. They all liked to eat out at the very finest restaurants – not just for a special occasion, but all of the time! Whenever I would see her off on another spending spree, I have to admit I couldn't help thinking *"But that's not your money to spend – it's the investors' money for the business."*

But that was how things went on, John off on his 'business trips' to find yet more investors who would be impressed by the black powder product and they would hand over huge amounts of money to him, and he would return home to hand it to his mother, who would spend it on a ridiculously lavish lifestyle for them, with apparently no thought to the business, or to the poor unsuspecting people who had 'invested' their hard-earned cash.

It all felt strangely wrong and nothing really added up, but who was I to comment? Young, naïve, with no real life experiences – so I didn't see it was my place to question other people or to see fault in them. I had no previous knowledge of how businesses ran, so I assumed perhaps this was what happened . . . and maybe it was just me being so innocent, seeing it in the wrong light? On the very odd occasion when

I did express any doubts, John was expert in convincing me things were fine.

Even when I really thought I needed to get out of all of this, the loneliness, the constant feeling of being shut out, the doubts about our financial situation, and John's strangely remote attitude to our marriage, I would consider the option. Go back to England? To what? I had given up college, I had announced to everyone I knew that this was to be my brave new world, that I had found happiness, that this was 'it'. No money, no home, no career. How humiliating would it be to go back, admit defeat, and ask for help?

And so I stayed.

Without doubt, the worst part of all this for me was definitely the very odd, tight-knit family life of John and his parents. Living with them, eating with them, going out for meals with them, having to ask for money, like a child asking for pocket money. And that feeling of being cut off from the outside world, no-one else allowed into the inner sanctum. They were so enmeshed with each other, it made me feel uncomfortable.

I once accidentally caught sight of a letter addressed to John from a former business associate of his. The writer was very angry with John over some business affairs that had gone wrong. I was shocked by this, but, when I asked about it, the family just brushed it off and said the chap was crazy. But I could tell that something was very wrong. John never wanted to go to Houston, or anywhere near, which I always found strange. It was clear that something had happened in Texas, enough to make him escape to the UK for a while, which is how we first met.

McAllen, our 'home', was a real 'back of beyond' place, not somewhere you'd expect a young family to live. It was the ideal place if you wanted to lay low for a while, and I often wondered if that was the case.

Life with the in-laws became so stifling for me, even though my husband obviously didn't see anything wrong with the set-up, I eventually persuaded him that we should move into a place of our own. Even then, they followed us and rented an apartment close by, so we still ate with them, spent time with them, and the three of them carried on with their cosy little get-togethers.

I honestly couldn't say, even now, what John thought marriage and family were all about, but he was never what you could call a good husband. And later, when the boys came along, he was a very absent father, never wanting to be 'hands-on', even when he was at home, which wasn't often.

Still accompanied by John's family, we moved to Houston. This is where I gave birth to our two beautiful sons – Joss was born in August 1988 and Michael followed in October 1989.

But, at least, there I could make some sort of life for myself. This was a big, cosmopolitan city and I made a lot of friends, especially through playing tennis, which I had always loved to do.

In the five years we spent as a family in Houston, I didn't really see much of my new husband. His time was devoured by business: he travelled extensively and had meetings all over the world. He was always setting up presentations, carrying out feasibility studies and poring over research material. And I wasn't part of any of this. I just got on with being a mother and looking after my two sons.

May 1990 arrived, and we moved home again – this time to Albuquerque, New Mexico, where life was to change dramatically . . .

We'd only been there for three months when John came home one day in an obviously agitated state. As he paced up and down the room, he told me *"everything's gone terribly wrong with the business . . . it's all disastrous . . . there's only one way out of this mess . . ."* and I listened, shocked and afraid. Then he added – as if he was telling me it might rain or that there was a good film on the TV – *"and by the way, I want a divorce."*

John had persuaded several influential people in Houston to give up their careers to join the business and – of course – to invest their own money in the expansion of the company and the production of the wonderful black powder. Some of these people had previously held very prestigious positions – one was a highly respected lawyer! They all gave up their lives in Houston and moved their families to Albuquerque, only to find the money had run out and there was no business, no miracle product, and no secure future.

Needless to say, they all lost every penny of their 'investment'. One chap was bankrupted, having risked all of his family wealth. They all had to move back to Houston and try to re-build their lives. They did take legal action and there ensued a lengthy court battle but I don't think they ever got any of their money back. I'm not sure what the end result was . . . but I felt so dreadful for them all.

Being totally honest, the marriage had never really been what you'd call successful. He'd never been there and our relationship wasn't great. I knew it was over. I also knew I had to think about myself and my two babies. I had to make sure the boys and I could have a safe, secure future. So, when John then proceeded to explain what 'the only way out' was, I listened intently.

He told me that he was going to rejoin the CIA. He had an incredibly high IQ and I could easily believe he was the sort of man they chose to employ. He had left to work in the family business but now that was in dire straits, the CIA were offering to sort it out in exchange for his reinstatement and control of the business which would provide a plausible cover for their activities. The deal was that I had to sign some papers to release the business, and they would then pay him a salary of five thousand dollars a month, which he would hand over to me as maintenance payments. I would also get a lump sum of eighty thousand dollars as a deposit on a house for me and the boys.

"I need to go back to being an agent again . . . it's our only answer . . . you wouldn't want that lifestyle, I'd be away all the time and it would be too dangerous for you and the boys . . ." His words fell on me like shards of fragmented glass, cutting me to ribbons. My mind was racing. I had to get out of this nightmare in one piece and with my sons safe. He added *"the CIA will take over the house and use it as a safe house."* I was terrified. It sounded like the worst gangster movie ever made.

Now, call me stupid. Feel free. Believe me, I've called myself a whole lot worse than that since all of this unfolded. But the thought of being financially stable, not having to worry, being in a position to support the three of us without a husband – this was my peace of mind. I had to focus on the future now.

John couldn't get rid of me and the children quickly enough, and I went to stay with the in-laws in Houston, where I consulted a lawyer about the signing of the document to release the business. Of course, I couldn't mention the CIA or any of that – John made it clear I would be in the worst possible danger if I did. The lawyer advised me not to sign: John had warned me that this would happen – obviously – but he was adamant that the CIA needed the papers signing or the deal would be off. No cash, no support, and possibly a whole truck-load of trouble. The lawyer was stalling as he could see I shouldn't be doing this. The bills were mounting, I was living with the people I most wanted to get away from, so I did what I had to do. I looked in the Yellow Pages and found a new lawyer. The papers were quickly signed, and I was free to return to England.

With the passing years, I think I began to understand John's haste in sending us off. He had to change everything in his life as quickly as possible. He remarried – his fourth wife – within months. I also lived to rue the day I ignored the advice of the first lawyer, who said the whole thing was rubbish, that I shouldn't sign, and he actually said he would bet on it that John would remarry quickly. He also warned me that the financial support wouldn't last long.

I would come to learn that he couldn't have been more accurate. But I was scared, totally unsure of the future, and I was running out of money with no prospect of any income. I had to put my two babies first – their security, their future – and I just had to ignore his advice. After all, it was simply advice.

On the flight back to England I mentally relived the ridiculous saga that had just enveloped me like some surrealist four-dimensional film. I couldn't believe what my life had become. I shuddered and held the boys close to me.

Back in Wimbledon, I rented a house close to my father, somewhere I felt safe and protected from all the madness, the fear, the worry. The sheer insanity of the previous weeks.

Chapter two

broken promises

A document dated the fourth of January 1991, worded in the coldly unemotional language of the legal domain, declares to the world that our marriage of less than eight years was over. Nine years from when we met, when life had seemed so full of hope, promise, a whole new future – all gone.

> *"It is, therefore, considered by this Court, and so ordered, adjudged and decreed by the Court, that the bonds of Matrimony heretofore existing between John C Proctor, Jr., Plaintiff, and Pamela Helen Proctor, Defendant, be and the same are here now and forever dissolved, cancelled and annulled."*

I was once more a single woman, but this time with two very small children, babies who were relying on me for everything.

That same document ordered the child support payments to me from John Proctor:

> *"It is Decreed that John C Proctor, Jr., pay to Pamela Proctor child support in the amount of $5,000.00 per month . . . Until the date any child reaches the age of 21 or is otherwise emancipated, or upon the death of the parent obligated*

to support the children . . . If Pamela Proctor should
remarry, the child support shall be reduced to $3,000.00
per month . . . John C Proctor, Jr., shall also pay for all
charges for tuition, books, registration fees, room and board,
and any other charges necessary for the children to attend
a public or private university or college, jointly selected
by the parties . . .'

The lump sum of eighty thousand dollars, part of the agreement
when I signed over my rights to the business, which was
supposed to help me buy a property in the UK where the boys
and I would live, never materialised. And even the promised
– and court ordered – regular maintenance payments of five
thousand dollars a month were only paid for the first six months
– then nothing.

In May 1991 the money stopped coming through and was
never to re-appear. In the July of that year, Edward and I began
our relationship and he – wonderful man that he is – started
to support the family.

John Proctor (I'll refer to him as JP from this point) married
his fourth wife in the August of the same year and it was then
that the words of that lawyer rang in my ears. He had been
absolutely right about the money, and he was right about JP
remarrying quickly.

The boys flew to the States for a three-week holiday in the
summer of 1993 with their father and his new wife, Tess. In
August of the same year, the child support agreement was
revised and the payment was reduced to nine hundred dollars
a month – but because JP was not paying anyway and I knew
he had no intention of paying, this mattered little to me.

In June 1994 Edward and I were married and it would
appear that everyone was moving on, getting on with their
new lives. JP and Tess moved from Houston to New Mexico
in the July and the next year he came over to London and

saw the boys while he was there. The boys began visiting their father for Christmas holidays in 1996 and this became an annual trip for them; I felt it was important for them to share such a special time of year with their father because it wasn't practical – or financially viable for us – to send them on such a journey at very regular intervals.

In August 1997 a letter arrived from Texas, addressed to all of us – myself, Edward and the boys. The content of this letter – extremely apologetic and overly explanatory – included information about his business situation, as well as a whole collection of reasons and excuses as to why he had not been sending me the maintenance payments for so long. He began rambling about some premises he had found for the business, going into ridiculous detail about this place, where he imagined they could build a production plant, offices, laboratories – and even living quarters for him and his current wife. The location sounded idyllic – not quite where you'd expect to stumble upon a big, smelly, fume-belching agrochemical plant – and he wrote of the *"incredible ambience"* of the place as *"a mountain valley with majestic vistas complete with deer, elk, Canadian geese and eagles"*. Did he really think I would be in the slightest bit interested in such things? Did he also really think he'd ever be given permission to site a fume-belching chemical plant in such a lovely area of natural beauty?

Over the seven A4 pages he waxed lyrical about his marvellous business plan, more new investors who then dropped out for whatever reasons, bank loans to the company that never materialised . . . how he and his wife (number four) were having to live with her parents, the tangles of litigation, job offers he'd had but never actually taken up, how things had gone badly wrong, and how completely broke he was – he was obviously attempting to gain my sympathy!

Then came the promises of reinstating the payments – and even his solemn word to repay Edward for all he had done to support the family. *"Edward, I know you have been a real champion during this whole protracted process and I want to compensate you financially for your sacrifices on behalf of the boys beyond what is owed to Pamela for child support. Pamela, I have a proposal for you and Edward that I believe can help to make amends for your hardships . . ."* It's a shame his word was never worth any more than the paper upon which it was written. Just as it's a shame that court ordered payments by children's fathers don't seem to be mandatory.

Last – but *most definitely* not least – he expressed his overwhelming desire to have the boys go to live with him in Texas: *"Most importantly, I want my boys to come and live with us for a while . . . I am their Father and I think we need to be together. We've spent a long enough time apart."* He reasoned this request by adding *"for a while to give you a chance to start on your own affairs."*

Given that Edward and I had, by now, been married for over three years and had been together for a total of six years, this sudden concern that we should have the opportunity to 'start on our own affairs' was a very poor façade to cover what JP was really plotting, but we couldn't possibly have known there was anything devious hidden in those words, not at the time.

The part of the letter addressed to Edward and myself ended with the promise *"I'll explain everything about my proposal when I see you in September."*

The last page was a letter to the boys, telling them how he missed them so much and wanted them with him, promising them gifts of things he knew they valued and wanted, and explaining how he was working to make enough money to send them to the best universities and buy them everything they would need. The content is sickly, it is not the type of letter you would write to small children, and you don't have to read between the lines to see the attempts to influence the boys . . .

"Dear Boys,

Daddy is very sorry for not calling or writing like I promised. This has been a difficult time for DAD. I lost my job and all my money due to some very bad luck the day after you went back to England. Daddy has been working very hard to overcome that bad luck and to make enough money so that I can fulfil my promises to your Mom, send you to the best universities and buy you two and your little brother what you need . . .

I hope one of these days when you get older you will understand and forgive Dad for not being with you . . .

My hard work and your patience will be finally rewarded. The war I've had with the bad guys for five long years is finally over. Daddy won and I can now take Pappy's and my technology and build a business for all of us.

Joss, I'll bring your birthday presents when I come plus the stuff I promise you both from Christmas – the lab coat for Michael and the karate outfit for Joss.

Joss, dad has a very big surprise for you when you come to the USA regarding Kung Fu and Karate.

Michael, remember our talk in the truck when we went to town . . .'

And so on.

When I read that letter now, knowing what his real reasons were for wanting the boys to be with him, it makes me sick to my stomach that any father of young children can lie so despicably to those children.

Needless to say, nothing promised in that whole outpouring ever came to fruition. He didn't visit that September, he didn't repay Edward in any way, no gifts arrived for the boys . . . I told him the boys could not go to live in Texas with him, but that they could visit for holidays. And it was after my rejection of this request that the alienation began.

In hindsight, I started to notice that something strange was happening with the boys after their Christmas visit to Texas in 1997. It was only much later, of course – too late for me to do anything about it – that I realised this must have been the beginning of JP's campaign of evil. They would speak to each other – and to him – in a sort of code language, and make odd little gestures with their fingers to each other, sharing secrets from which I was always excluded.

It made me feel somewhat uncomfortable, but, given our circumstances, I put this down to the 'all boys together' aspect of having two sons who spent very little time with their father and sharing these special little games between the three of them seemed to be perhaps their way of keeping a close relationship with their absent parent. Surely any mother would not bear a grudge over such behaviour?

Chapter three

two little boys – my son Joss

I think most people would agree that a senior paediatrician is
certainly someone to be taken seriously in matters of child
health. Dr J. Wyatt was that someone. At the time he was the
Senior Community Paediatrician for Dorset Healthcare and,
on the eleventh of June 1998, he wrote a letter to a Dr Copple,
Consultant Paediatrician at Poole Hospital, asking him to see
my son Joss following a request from Joss' school as there was
"concern about his fine motor skills". Dr Wyatt mentions the fact
that I had flagged up certain issues concerning Joss, such as
*"of probably greater concern to mother is poor concentration. Joss
was reported at his first school as having poor concentration which
they expected would improve with time. Mother feels that this
remains a significant problem."* The letter goes on to say
*"Nevertheless, Joss' history seems to indicate quite strongly a
dyspraxic problem, apart from his reported clumsiness with certain
hand/co-ordination tasks, he has poor concentration and very poor
organisational skills."*

Dr Wyatt received a reply from Dr Copple's registrar, Dr
Rebecca Harris, dated the twenty-second of September 1998,
thanking Dr Wyatt for the referral of *"this very pleasant
ten-year-old boy"* and reporting that *"his lack of concentration
affects his progress in all subjects . . . He actually has private English*

lessons and on one-to-one with this teacher his concentration is good . . . Joss is able to ride a bicycle well and had no problem acquiring this skill . . . Joss has no problems with his behaviour. He is dry by day and night. Joss enjoys playing on his computer and going out on his bicycle with his friends . . . He had one febrile convulsion when he was three years of age[1] . . . On assessment at three years of age at St George's he was within the normal range for development . . . Examination of the cardiovascular, respiratory and abdominal systems were normal. His blood pressure today was 90/60. He had no cutaneous stigmata. Full examination of the cranial nerves and peripheral nervous system was normal . . . It appears that Joss may well have attention deficit disorder without the hyperactivity . . . I will also contact Joss' school for further information on Joss and for a Conners' teacher rating scale to be completed."

The letter concludes with an arrangement for a review in six weeks' time when Dr Harris would be able to make a decision as to whether Joss had ADD (Attention Deficit Disorder) and if he would benefit from medical treatment.

On the thirteenth of November 1998 Dr Harris wrote to Dr B Lee at Wimborne surgery to confirm that she had reviewed Joss in clinic on that day and that he had shown to be above average for the ADD index and inattention problems. She states *"we have discussed medication today in clinic and we are going to try Joss on a trial of Ritalin medication"* and asks Wimborne surgery to continue to provide repeat prescriptions after the six-week prescription she had supplied. Her diagnosis stated in this letter was *"Attention deficit disorder"*.

On the fourth of December 1998 Dr S Morgan, Specialist Registrar in Community Paediatrics to Dr Copple at Poole Hospital, wrote to the Wimborne surgery to advise that I had reported *"that he is more responsive, more articulate and alert,*

---

1   *The febrile convulsion was the result of an extremely high temperature while Joss was suffering with an ear infection when he was three years old.*

keener to participate in events and more switched on" and that Joss' English teacher had agreed that Joss was more responsive and that it was *"like a veil had been lifted"*. Dr Morgan commented that *"this is obviously very pleasing and I would hope that progress is maintained."*

In the second and final paragraph of her letter, Dr Morgan advises that the medication prescribed – Methylphenidate ten milligrams in the morning and ten milligrams at lunchtime – *"is effective for a year or possibly two years but no very convincing proof that it is effective in the long term."*

The letter ends with an arrangement for Dr Morgan to see Joss again in three months.

The above is very important in that it paints a picture of a normal child who has a health problem and who is receiving excellent medical attention from professionals, a child whose mother is aware of certain issues and has taken steps to have those issues examined, a child whose medical experts and whose school are working together with an exchange of information so as to help everyone concerned get to the bottom of the issues and deal with them in the most appropriate manner.

The above explains that the professionals involved in my son's healthcare made a diagnosis of ADD based on thorough and careful testing, discussion, reporting and sharing of information with other appropriate professionals.

The above does not paint a picture of anything other than that.

my son Michael

Michael was what you would call a really normal child; he was easy-going, sociable – not a shy boy at all. At school, for all of the time he was with me, he was very popular with the other kids and always had lots of friends around him.

Academically, he didn't stand out either way, but was average in class across all of his subjects – which I think is good because it means he was well-rounded and capable of dealing with things generally.

Michael took part in all of the school's sports activities – football, rugby, tennis and so on. He really enjoyed his golf and tennis and played almost every day after school, which I encouraged because it was reassuring to see him out in the fresh air getting healthy exercise instead of sitting at home in front of a computer, which seems all too typical of children these days.

He had a really close relationship with myself and Edward, which was a wonderful reflection of how caring and fatherly Edward was towards the boys. Another fond memory is of Michael and Edward walking the dog by the river every evening, Michael wheeling his bike along the way.

We were really just an unremarkable, average family getting on with life until this dreadful nightmare began.

Chapter four

our new arrival

A year or so after we were married, Edward and I made a huge decision. The boys were older now, life was nicely settled and we knew that we would spend the rest of our lives together. Edward had never had children, so we decided to have a child of our own. The prospect of a new addition to the family was a very happy one. As with such things, babies will only come along when the time is right and we did have to wait for three years, even though there was nothing medically wrong. At last, in March, 1999, our new baby, Daniella, came into the world.

Little did we know it then, but having her was one of the few things that would later give me a reason to keep going, to merely survive, when life took a hellish turn less than a year later.

Chapter five

Christmas, 1999

Their father was due to be in London on business and so the plan was for us to take the boys to meet up with him at Gatwick, then they would all travel together to the States for their Christmas holiday.

I was packing suitcases and getting everything ready for their trip when I suddenly realised Joss' passport had expired. Panic! I rang JP straight away and – in his usual style of having to be in control of all things – he said he had 'friends in high places' at Continental Airlines and could pull some strings to sort the passport issue. (The man is so full of his own importance, he didn't even notice the pun.) He called back later, presumably after speaking to his high-flying friends, to say it was absolutely impossible and that we would have to go to the American Embassy to obtain an extension on the passport expiry date. He added that the Embassy would be open on the Sunday (really? A government building?). Of course, we drove to Grosvenor Square and, sure enough, it was closed.

I couldn't possibly have known at the time why this was, but JP really didn't want us to go to the airport to meet him for some reason, and he tried very hard to convince us not to go. But I was determined to grab the opportunity to speak to him about how the business was doing because he owed us so much in unpaid child support. And so we did all meet up at Gatwick. We had little Dani with us and, while we were all in McDonalds, I had to pop off for a while to change her, so we weren't all together for very long, but I did notice that JP's behaviour was very odd. He was most noticeably avoiding eye contact with me and he seemed incredibly uncomfortable. He did manage to spend about ten minutes or so alone with the boys. Eventually, he went off, leaving us to resolve the passport problem – which, as it turned out, was not a problem. Edward decided to approach someone from BA and they directed him to the Continental desk where he explained what had happened. The response was *"Oh, yes, this happens a lot"*, and a few phone calls later it was all sorted.

We were relieved as this meant we wouldn't have to hang around London for days on end, and we could go back home. We stayed overnight with Edward's mother and put the boys on a flight the next day.

I will always remember my boys' little faces as we said goodbye, and I will never stop regretting letting them go on that fateful trip.

It was New Year's Eve when I first sensed trouble. I had telephoned to speak to the boys and Tess answered. For some reason, I didn't like the tone of her voice. Then she said she thought the boys had been neglected and mistreated. I really didn't like what I was hearing so I told her I would be on the first available flight the next day to pick them up, then I hung up to begin arranging the flights. Hardly five minutes later, she called back and spoke very nicely to me, saying everything was fine.

Much later, I would realise that the reason for this sudden change of attitude was that this was the thirty-first of December and they hadn't yet acquired their Temporary Custody Order

– which would be granted on the sixth of January. If I had been so upset I had actually flown out to bring the boys back, that would have completely scuppered their entire plan.

If only I had known what was to follow.

With the festivities past and the first new year of the new century just beginning, I was almost due to pick the boys up from the airport when the phone rang. It was a phone call that would change our lives in the most appalling and incomprehensible way. I remember it was eleven o'clock at night, UK time, on January the ninth. The drawling American accent was that of JP's lawyer – or should I say, his friend who happened to be a lawyer. His voice expressed no emotion whatsoever as he told me the boys would not be returning to England, that they were staying in the States . . .

"Mrs Roche, don't come to the airport on Thursday, they won't be there. Joss and Michael are not coming back and you need to get a lawyer."

My heart was pounding, my mind went into overdrive. I screamed and screamed until I could barely breathe. Edward rushed into the room, fear and concern etched in his face. I was sobbing, choking, shaking, as the words tumbled out, repeating the unbelievable message I had just heard. Neither of us could take it in. The happiness life had just recently given us was suddenly, in one blink of an eye, wrenched from me. What on earth was happening? What was John Proctor up to? It had to be something awful – but why were the boys not coming home? So many questions tumbling around in my head . . . and no answers.

Then, a second call, this time the most welcome sound of my son's voice: Joss said *"Mummy, we want to stay here. Don't worry, mummy, daddy says he's going to fly you out in the holidays to see us.*" For some reason, this did not put my mind at rest.

In simple terms, my ex-husband was refusing to return the children to us and it was obviously up to me, as their mother and the parent who had custody, to fight him to get them back, whatever that meant. We had no idea how to deal with this situation – something thrust upon us with no prior warning – but all I knew was this was very wrong and I wanted my boys back with me, with our family, where they belonged.

Chapter six

the battle begins

All I could think to do was ring absolutely everyone in the family. It didn't matter that it was now the middle of the night – there was something here far more important. I had no sleep that night and the following few days were a nightmare waiting game to see what would happen next.

My sister-in-law, a very efficient lady who is far better informed than I am, contacted the Foreign Office on our behalf and they advised us to speak to the Lord Chancellor's Office where such matters were dealt with. An appointment was made for us to meet with them at their Westminster offices. That meeting brought welcome relief, just knowing that we were speaking to people in official positions who had knowledge of something that we were finding totally alien. We were told about the Hague Convention and how it was the law in such cases of parental abduction, within those countries who had adopted it. Fortunately, both the UK and the United States were member states. This was such good news – it made me feel safe, it was our beacon of hope. Knowing nothing about any of the laws surrounding our situation, I assumed that the Hague Convention would be watertight.

The Hague, in the Netherlands, is the International

Centre for Justice and Peace. In 1980 the *Hague Convention on the Civil Aspects of International Child Abduction* became law.

Acting for all of its member states, the Hague Conference declared that:

". . . the interests of children are of paramount importance in matters relating to their custody"

and that it was:

"desiring to protect children internationally from the harmful effects of their wrongful removal or retention and to establish procedures to ensure their prompt return to the State of their habitual residence, as well as to secure protection for rights of access."

In the event of one parent contravening a custody agreement by holding the child in their keeping following an access visit, the Hague Convention requires the child to be returned immediately to the country where the original custody agreement was ordered. This is Article 3 of the Convention:

"The removal or the retention of a child is to be considered wrongful where it is in breach of rights of custody attributed to a person, an institution or any other body, either jointly or alone, under the law of the State in which the child was habitually resident immediately before the removal or retention . . ."

I was desperate to ask the question, *"Would the boys automatically be sent back to the UK?"* and the lady replied *"In most cases"*. Her words jarred on my mind for an instant – why not *all* cases? But, just as quickly, the relief of learning about this powerful legal precedent that must be followed by both countries took over again.

The most vitally important thing was that we must arrange to have legal representation by someone in the vicinity of where the court hearing was to take place. Neither Edward nor I knew any lawyers over there, and this was such a hugely important decision. All we could do was listen to the advice we were being given. The Lord Chancellor's Office people carried out a search on their computer and found a list of lawyers who handled Hague Convention cases in New Mexico. It wasn't an extensive list but the one they suggested to us was David Waters.

One day short of three sleepless weeks later, we were in a courtroom in New Mexico. This was the Hague Convention Trial. The twenty-ninth of January in the year 2000. It all felt surreal, a terrifying nightmare that would surely end abruptly any second . . . but it didn't. There was no such respite. This was the beginning of thirteen long years of hell on earth . . .

David Waters, of David Waters Associates, was based in Santa Fe. He had experience of Hague Convention cases, which was reassuring. His fees were three hundred and fifty dollars an hour plus his secretary's time, which was an additional eighty dollars an hour: we immediately sent him a retainer of ten thousand dollars. The total bill was about fifteen thousand dollars plus expenses. Bear in mind, this was 1999.

Although relating monetary cost to anything around the safety, well-being and happiness of children is, at least, distasteful, I have to mention here my absolute gratitude that I was in a position to access such finances.

My father has always been the most generous man I know, and he gladly paid for all of the hefty legal bills, the psychologists' and other professionals' reports, the airline tickets back and forth – and his wedding gift to Edward and me was his house in Wimborne. My father had never been at all happy about me marrying JP and he was proved absolutely right to have such doubts. He wanted to do whatever he could to help me get his grandchildren back where they belonged.

There are people who find themselves in a similar position but who simply cannot afford to pay legal costs on this scale, air fares around the world, hotel bills, and so on. These people have no option but to accept their fate and lose their child or children without ever being able to do anything about it.

It is an expensive battle to fight, and this is so wrong it disgusts me.

A document date-stamped the nineteenth of January, 2000, entitled *Plaintiff's Brief Supporting Complaint For Return Of Her Children Under The Hague Convention On Child Abduction*, was filed in the District Court of New Mexico.

The Plaintiff – that was me. I was contesting the injunction that had been granted to JP by asking the court to take note that the retention of children *"from their habitual residence is wrongful under the Hague Convention and the Act[2] if a person in the residential country is exercising custody rights to the child at the moment of retention in the non-residential country. In this case it is undisputed that the plaintiff has had custody of her two minor children in England pursuant to a custody order entered in Texas 1991. The defendant retained the children in New Mexico and failed to return them at an agreed upon time, January 9, 2000, after a Christmas visitation in New Mexico."*

The Summary of my Brief included reference to the Precedent Case of Friedrich vs. Friedrich, as follows:

"The authorities are clear that the Convention and the Act protect children internationally from the harmful effects of their wrongful removal or retention and establish procedures

---

2   *The International Child Abduction Remedies Act*, found at 42 USC §§ 11601–11610.

to ensure their prompt return to the state of their habitual residence. By operation of the Convention, 'a United States District Court has the authority to determine the merits of an abduction claim, but not the merits of the underlying custody claim'. Friedrich vs. Friedrich, 983 F.2d 1396, 1400 (6th Cir. 1993). (Friedrich I) It is also well established that the defenses in the act are 'narrow' and are not the basis for avoiding return of a child merely because an American court believes it can better or more quickly resolve a dispute. Thus, the defendant must not only establish the defense of grave risk of harm by clear and satisfactory evidence, but he must establish that the country of habitual residence is unable to give the children adequate protection. Friedrich vs. Friedrich, 78 F.3d 1060, 1067 (6th Cir. 1996). (Friedrich II). In this case the courts of England are as able to give the children in question adequate protection there, as would be the New Mexico court, had defendant made his custody motion in England. As such, the policy of the Convention and the Act requires defendant's issues to be resolved in the courts of England, the jurisdiction of the children's habitual residence."

My aim was, obviously, to demonstrate to the court by referring to the precedent case where it was made clear, that the case should be heard in the courts of the country where the children normally resided – in my case, since I had custody of the children and I lived in England, in the courts of England.

Chapter seven

nightmare in court

Because our case was international, Mr Waters had arranged for the hearing to take place in the Federal Court in Albuquerque, rather than the local county court. Presiding was Judge Connor, a man approaching his sixtieth year, a man who – we later discovered – had never heard an ordinary custody case, and who was certainly not at all familiar with the Hague Convention. So, moving the case up to a higher court was actually working against us, rather than giving us more hope of success.

Keen to provide him with everything that could have even the faintest impact on the proceedings, I had given Mr Waters photos of the boys, letters from friends and neighbours in England, and the letter from JP in which he made it very clear that he wanted the boys to live with him. The letter that also included mention of the unpaid child support. But Waters was so confident that the case would in no way become protracted or complex, he dismissed all of this as unnecessary. Looking back, he seemed to put far more thought into choosing which designer briefcase to take with him to court.

We spent that night in an inexpensive local hotel, where I actually admit to sleeping much better than of late, encouraged by the existence of this suave attorney who seemed almost nonchalant, so confident of a good outcome.

The next morning, we met with him at his hotel – one of the most luxurious around – and over breakfast we discussed what we should expect and how things would proceed, before heading off for the courthouse.

The Federal Court House on Gold Avenue in the centre of Albuquerque is a most imposing structure. A sky-rise, clinically modern and as austere as one would expect. Once inside, we noted there were armed police stationed all around. As we passed through Security, we spotted the Proctors following behind us with Michael and Joss. My heart leapt and I smiled at the boys, but – to my horror – they recoiled and hid from me. I sensed so strongly – *I knew* – that something was going on and it was not good. I had no way of knowing what.

In the courtroom, JP's lawyer, a rather creepy man so obviously inexperienced in handling custody cases, quite bizarrely approached us and tried to shake hands with us. We declined, appalled at this lack of basic respect. This was Michael Bolton, personal friend of JP's. I doubt very much if he was ever paid for his services. Right from the outset, he was reprimanded by the judge for not standing up when addressing the court. His behaviour, demeanour and court protocol were all sadly inept. And yet, none of this proved to be at all detrimental – in fact, the judge actually started helping him when he floundered. It was unbelievable. The whole experience evolved into a nightmare farce and, as it did so, things went more and more in their favour.

In another life, JP's performance in the courtroom could have won him an Oscar. He had obviously prepared for this day incredibly well, in minute detail and leaving nothing to chance.

He even brought out a chap who, we later found out, worked for him, declaring this man to be a 'long-standing friend' of his. In his late fifties, not particularly groomed, and wearing denim jeans and tee-shirt, Bill Krantz looked like someone out of a spoof hill-billy sketch. He claimed he organised fishing trips to Alaska. However inappropriate he appeared, the judge claimed he was the only non-biased witness present, and so took on board everything this man said.

This made me inwardly furious, since my own brother, our only witness, was not allowed to take the stand – because he was deemed to be biased! The frustration of this was enormous and hard to cope with.

Krantz told the court that he accompanied JP to the airport to collect the boys and said they were in a shocking state – overweight, improperly clothed with no socks on, dirty, beaten and abused. He said later they all went out for something to eat and the boys began pouring out how they had been abused and badly treated in England; he said it was so awful other people actually got up and left the restaurant.

I still find it unbelievable that no-one questioned this: if you found your children in such a state as described by JP and his trusted 'friend', why on earth would you then take them to a restaurant, a public place . . . why would you not take them straight home where this alleged 'state' could be dealt with in privacy, in the safety of their familiar surroundings? And why would you take with you a work colleague, someone not even in the family, someone the children didn't know?

Add to this, referring back to when JP met us all at the airport at Christmas 1999, if he had seen, or even suspected, the 'appalling condition' of the boys when he met us, why did he then go off, leaving them with us – the people he apparently by then regarded as their abusers – leaving them to stay until we could manage to get them on a flight, which turned out to be the following day but he couldn't have known it wouldn't take longer, especially since this was the Christmas holiday period. How could he be assured that we would, in fact, send them? Who, in their right mind, would do that if they had even the slightest suspicion of mistreatment?

49

JP had also been getting some 'professionals' on side – completely without our knowledge he had taken the boys to see a psychologist, Charlotte McKay, PhD, at the end of December. She had interviewed the boys, both with and without JP present, and she had written her report – all without my knowledge, without any contact with me, and without any request for medical, school or family records from the UK. Wearing a dark navy blue business suit, blonde hair cut short, this woman took the stand and I glowered at her across the room. How dare she give such credence to the Proctors' claims when she had only just met them and had not spoken so much as one single word to me – the custodial parent for ten years, the mother of these children. How on earth could this be allowed? How could it be legal?

And yet it was.

And, as her report unfolded, there were so many glaring inconsistencies, so many questions that *begged* to be asked – and yet no-one else there batted an eye.

> "When Mr Proctor initiated this referral, he stated that he was very concerned about unsolicited statements made by Joss and Michael regarding various incidents of maltreatment by their stepfather, Edward Roche. He also reported that these statements are consistent with statements the boys had made on their previous visit."

If the boys had, indeed, reported any of this type of 'abuse' – or any cruelty, violence or other mistreatment – on their previous visit, which was one year earlier, why on earth did JP do nothing at that time? Why did he leave his two young, vulnerable children with people he allegedly viewed at the time as abusers? Surely, any normal father would have to take action right away, especially given that the children lived so far from him that he was unable to monitor events closely, was unable to pop round to rescue them quickly if they needed help?

But the court just sat and took all of JP's lies on board, unquestioning. It made me wonder if there was a bigger, unseen plan lurking somewhere, a plan that all of these people were a party to, and nothing we said or did was going to make a scrap of difference.

> *"Events they described included being 'kicked up the stairs', being hit repeatedly with the buckle end of a belt, slapped in the face, and slammed into the wall."*

The boys both had an excellent attendance record at school. If they had ever been treated in this way, the school staff would have noticed physical marks, behavioural changes, or something that would have flagged up a warning and we would have been called in for a meeting. Or, if things had been half as bad as this report suggested, surely social services would have been pounding on our door at some point?

No-one even thought to mention these aspects and, again, it was all taken as read.

> *". . . and their report of other people who witnessed or knew about their abuse."*

Other people? What other people? People who *knew* about this completely fabricated abuse? Where were they? Where were their statements? Surely this would be a crucial element of JP's case? This must be legally mandatory in such a case?

No-one was in the slightest bit concerned to know who these other 'people' were, what they had to say, or even the details of what it was they were supposed to have witnessed. Apart from the fishing trip organiser, slash, best friend of JP, obviously no witnesses were needed. And yet, included in this woman's report was the admission *"Although there was no way to verify Michael and Joss' allegations . . ."* – so in one paragraph she tells of witnesses to the abuse, and in another paragraph she says there is no way to verify anything. Excuse me, I'm no legal expert, and I'm certainly not a psychologist, but here's an idea. Ask the 'witnesses'. Surely, that would be sufficient verification – or not.

"Both children reported that incidents such as those described here occur almost daily."

Daily abuse, daily violence towards children, would – without a shred of doubt – leave some marks, bruises, scars. No-one asked if the boys had been examined for such marks, or if there were any medical evidence to support these claims of physical mistreatment. No-one demanded that their school be contacted for any information.

". . . Joss has 'fits' where he bangs his head and cries."

If anyone had cared to look at earlier UK medical records on the boys, they would have known instantly about poor Joss' history: when he was three, the febrile convulsion he had suffered, brought on by a very high temperature following an ear infection. Later, the slight delay in his motor skills and the subsequent testing at St George's Hospital. In June 1998, when he was referred for assessment, he was subsequently seen and tested thoroughly by a Senior Community Paediatrician and two Specialist Paediatric Registrars, in NHS clinics and hospitals. Then, after much testing and consultation, Joss was prescribed methylphenidate (Ritalin) and, after about four weeks of medication, he was more responsive, more articulate and generally more 'switched on'.

Then, the cherry sitting atop this marvellously professional cake, she concludes: *"Obviously, these interviews do not constitute a complete evaluation nor an inquiry adequate to state conclusively that Michael and Joss Proctor have suffered abuse by their stepfather. However, it is my opinion that their reporting is credible enough and the circumstances described serious enough to conclude that there is a likelihood that the boys are at risk and to warrant a more intensive investigation prior to allowing their return to England."*

Our lawyer questioned JP. The man had an answer for everything, and he was so slick it was sickening. I think Waters was taken aback by the very well prepared ambush. I repeatedly asked him to read out the letter that JP had sent us, as evidence that JP's intention was to have the children to live with him. Having previously disregarded the letter, believing it would not be necessary, Waters now tried to use it to pull the case back in our favour. The letter also mentioned the unpaid child support, which I desperately thought would help, but no, this case was not about child support so the mention of it was dismissed out of hand. We were reminded that this case was about abuse, nothing else. The letter made no difference. No matter what our lawyer tried, he was being met with a brick wall at every turn.

My turn. Stomach doing somersaults, dry choking in my throat. Judge Connor asked me about the clothes the boys had been wearing, and had they been wearing any socks on the plane? In my head, I was shouting *"What the hell has this to do with socks, you moron? This is my children we are talking about!"* I answered his questions. He then asked me what I thought was happening here. Strange question. Knowing nothing of the recognised form of abuse which this later proved itself to be, I simply told him I believed JP had been *getting into the boys' minds*. So, even without the proper knowledge, I realised this was something to do with mind distortion, controlling what the children perceived and believed.

And, thanks to this 'professional' woman's damning report, the bottom line was that the boys would now be kept in the States for re-evaluation before being allowed to return to

England. What should have happened was the boys should have been sent home immediately, with an escort. Social services in the UK would then carry out a thorough inspection of the case, including interviews with schools, GP, neighbours, family members and so on until they had a bigger picture from which they could assess what was really going on and how it should be dealt with. The US judge would have been formally advised of the outcome.

The idea that the boys could remain even longer with their father – no, he doesn't deserve that title – with that monster, that evil, manipulative, unfeeling monster who could even contemplate causing this devastation to his own sons, to their mother, to family . . . this was so dangerous, leaving them in his 'care' so that he could work on their little minds even more, do even more damage.

We would later find out that this re-evaluation was to take nine months and would drag us into an extremely costly and difficult court case in the States.

As if we weren't already feeling totally alienated – we were so far from home, surrounded by people we didn't know, trying to deal with something that had hit us like a runaway train, feeling this awful sense of dread as we saw the case slipping away from us, completely impotent to do anything about it – there was this strangely unprofessional performance by, it seemed, everyone involved. It was like the blackest comedy sketch and it was not making us laugh.

Let me enlighten you with a few extracts – and I assure you they are taken straight from the court transcript, unamended . . .

JP's lawyer: *May I approach the witness?*
The Court: *Well, you can. Are you going to ask him some more about what England does over there?*

JP's lawyer: *No, sir.*
The Court: *Don't you think their setup is such that they could take care of these boys if they were . . . needed to?*
JP's lawyer: *I did until I did some research, and I'm absolutely convinced it's not very far from the worst third-world country, and I can . . . and I can . . . I believe I can establish their laws are so inadequate.*

And, shortly after that . . .

JP's lawyer: *Are you familiar with that* (document) *now that you've looked at it?*
Judge: *This is . . . sorry, this is a report from which court?*
JP's lawyer: *It says the European Court on Human Rights.*
Judge: *And is that a hearing under the treaty that you described earlier?*
JP's lawyer: *Yes, sir. Isn't that what it says on the top? It says Aid versus England?*

And a little later . . .

JP's lawyer: *. . . His attorney says, you better find out if these kids are trying to please you or whatever, get a professional to look at it. They went to a professional. The professional came back and says I had to file a complaint. . . . When you have five dots in a line, you have a line.*

What? It was so unbelievable, and yet it was real.

After this hearing was over, I tried to obtain a copy of the whole Hague Convention court transcript from the court reporter at the Federal Court House. Strangely, the entire record of this hearing had been redacted.

As I observed these strangers, as if watching a play that would surely end soon and I could return to reality . . . they seemed to be totally devoid of any interest or compassion as to the matters they were discussing, apparently disinterested in the knowledge that their decisions, their judgements, their opinions, would have life-changing consequences for those of us being discussed.

Their very manner, their appalling lack of clarity, of any professional stance – the entire scene was strangely surreal. They spoke as if in some stupid badly acted cowboy film, the lengthy drawling speech in constant mind-numbing monotone. They were asking each other questions and no-one seemed to have the answers. Crucial questions, points of law – their own law, the law they had surely studied and in which they had gained some degree of expertise, otherwise why were they here? How can these people be in control of something so desperately serious? It all beggared belief and all we could do was sit and listen, forced to watch this ridiculous farce unfold in front of us.

When one thinks of a court hearing in England, it is a matter of ultimate seriousness, everyone involved professional, learned, respectful, courteous. Points of law referred to and accurately recorded. All things clinical and precise.

This charade, this whatever-it-is, this unending nightmare that we have found ourselves caught up in, unable to wake, with no voice, no strength, no means of escape . . . this is surely not reality?

Then the judge announced that he was going to speak to the boys in his chambers. This felt so bad, it made my blood run cold – we had already seen how they had behaved towards me earlier, and there had been a telephone call just before this madness unfolded when the boys had spoken to me in the most inappropriate way . . . and now, together with that so-called professional woman's report, surely this could only go one way? This, I was now convinced, would be another nail in the coffin, and the corpse in that coffin was our hope of getting the boys back where they belonged.

In a matter of a few weeks, my two lovely sons had gone through the most dreadful transformation and now appeared to be as dehumanised as robots. The change in them was terrifying. Even my brother was shocked. They sat opposite us, clinging on to JP and Tess and making awful wailing noises. It all beggared belief.

The judge re-appeared and there was more hill-billy courtroom drama, then the proceedings were beginning to be wound up. I caught my breath as the judge read out his decision. Although it was agreed that JP had been wrong to withhold the children in the first place, now the judge had had chance to speak to the boys he believed they had been abused and therefore they should stay in the US with JP and Tess. That was the law, according to Clause 13b of the Hague Convention – the very document on which we had pinned all our hopes.

Clause 13b states that a child should *not* be returned:

"[if] there is a grave risk that his or her return would expose the child to physical or psychological harm or otherwise place the child in an intolerable situation."

Such bitter irony.

The same Clause also says:

"The judicial or administrative authority also may refuse to order a return of a child if the child objects to being returned and has attained an age and degree of maturity to take into account its views."

Age? What age? And who decides whether the child is sufficiently 'mature' or not? There are no specific details or guidelines set. Presumably this is all being left to the discretion of the individual judge in each case – a person who has known nothing whatsoever about the people involved or their lives before he sees them in court. How can anyone – however highly qualified – make such a judgement based on so very little knowledge?

I almost passed out. I was shaking and screaming *"They are my babies!"* over and over, as I was helped out of the courtroom by Edward and my brother. This was barbaric. Even knowing there were other people in the room, who had been allowed to sit in and observe, I couldn't contain myself. I didn't care. Nothing mattered.

I lost my children on that day and I lost a part of myself with them.

Chapter eight

realisation

The realisation was instantaneous, and it slammed through my mind like machine-gun fire. In a single moment, I could see clearly the answer to all of the little questions I'd accumulated in my head over the past two years. The secrets, the strange code language, the hand gestures to each other when I was around, the post-holiday complaints that Texas was so much better than England, the off-hand attitude towards me for a while following each trip . . . it all made some kind of hideous sense now.

For reasons I could not even begin to imagine yet, the boys' father had been turning them against me, indoctrinating them, poisoning their minds – to such an extent that my own children seemed to be utterly convinced – no! it was much, *much* worse than that! Dear God, they actually believed that Edward and I had caused them harm, hurt them incredibly – abused them. How on earth could anyone do this to their own little innocent children?

This knowledge was too much to bear and I kept telling myself I was being paranoid, that this could not possibly be true . . . my mind reeled with questions, visions, things I would suddenly remember, but I kept coming back to the same terrible conclusion. Even worse was to follow. Was it not enough that this man, who I now realised I had never known, had damaged my boys in this unbelievably hellish way? Apparently not. Having done his worst with them, having thoughtlessly and heartlessly destroyed their relationship with their own mother, having caused me so much heartache and grief I was barely hanging on to my sanity, he had somehow created a scenario around all of this evil that had obviously convinced the authorities that he was the good, honest, protective parent and that Edward and I were the awful perpetrators of these heinous crimes. He had applied to the court in New Mexico and had been granted an emergency protective order and temporary custody of the children. He had rallied the support of some dubious 'professionals' and he had created a world of evil around my boys, whose minds he was endangering beyond belief.

I cannot describe how it felt to have my children taken from me, made worse because one child's health was not yet one hundred per cent, a child who was perhaps not mentally strong enough to cope with what was happening here. I had already seen them both in the most awful state, I was in too much shock to think straight, I had no idea what had brought them to this point, and now I was being told I could not have them with me, could not look after them, make sure they were well and cared for.

This was a torture I felt I would not survive.

Chapter nine

home alone

We went into a small side room with Mr Waters. He gave me a hug, but I was inconsolable. He told us we had thirty days in which we could lodge an appeal, but his advice was not to try that. He said no judge in their right mind would send the children back to the UK in that condition, having witnessed just how bad they were. He admitted he was shocked by what he had seen.

He said the best thing we could do for now was to wait it out and see if, after a few months of life with dad, the novelty might wear off and they would probably start to miss me. They might see for themselves that the grass is not always greener, etcetera. That was being very optimistic, given what had just taken place. But I had absolutely no choice in the matter.

We booked into the Loretto Hotel in Santa Fe for the night. A luxury hotel, it was a beautiful adobe style place – quite the reverse of the one where we spent the previous night. We had dinner in the hotel restaurant and there was country and western music playing while people danced. Happy people, people enjoying life. It all passed me by.

After a few hours' sleep, I was awake at four o'clock, instantly crying and screaming as the harsh reality hit my brain. I leapt out of the bed, frantic and in a blind panic. The truth of what had happened was sinking in, now that the shock was subsiding. I threw up all over the beautifully tiled handbasin.

We flew home the next day. I could barely speak and Edward could say and do nothing to appease me. I wore a very big pair of sunglasses and, once on the plane, I buried my head in a pillow then, from the moment the plane lifted off from the runway, I cried non-stop for about six hours. I didn't care what the other passengers might think – I'd lay money on the fact that none of them had been through quite the same ordeal.

We landed on home soil to be greeted by a typical English January morning – cold, damp and miserable. My brother's wife met us at Paddington station and we all went back to their place in Maida Vale. I was shattered, jet-lagged and traumatised. I tried to get some sleep in one of their girls' bedrooms, but sleep evaded me. I curled up into the tightest ball I could and just cried again.

As I opened my swollen, stinging eyes, I caught sight of a tapestry wall hanging of an angel and, somehow, that comforted me a little. It made me think there has to be a higher power, some divine being who could intervene to rescue me and my children from this horror. This hell.

We stayed with them for a couple of days, just going over and over everything that had happened in the courtroom. I was still very much in shock and spent most of the time staring at the ceiling.

On our return to Wimborne, so many good friends and neighbours came flocking round to find out what our news was. Everyone was very supportive. People can be wonderful.

Chapter ten

rescue mission

The burning question, of course, was – what next?

Back in our own house, I was in such a state of emotional turmoil and exhaustion, I couldn't think clearly and yet my mind wouldn't switch off. I went into the boys' bedrooms and there, lying on their beds, were the South Park pencil cases I had bought for them to take to school for the new term. Most of their clothes still hanging in wardrobes, photos of them all around. Everything I saw was a symbol of what I had lost. It was all too upsetting.

Other children, friends of the boys, walking past the living-room window in their school uniforms . . . I just wanted to run away from this place where everything and everyone was a constant reminder and I could do absolutely nothing about any of it.

At that time, thank goodness for little Dani, for whom I simply had to keep going.

I had no intention of losing my children in silence, and certainly not because of a catalogue of lies and deceit. About a month passed by and the shock and trauma finally began to dissolve away, allowing me to regain strength of mind. I knew I was not going to give up. Desperately searching my memory and recalling everything that had happened, I tried to find some way, something I could use, something I could work on to get the boys back.

It must have been around March when I started to receive the most venomous letters from Michael Bolton, blaming us for the deterioration in Joss' mental health. That hurt me dreadfully, to know that my son was having a mental breakdown and I was so far away, was unable to go to him, to help him. Even just to hold him. Being blamed for the illness made it so much worse for us.

The deterioration in Joss' mental health, which we were being accused of bringing about, took the form of him exhibiting psychotic behaviour – to the extent that hospitalisation was recommended. This meant he had to leave the school he had been attending and was placed in a home-school programme. His father took him to see a Dr Rene Gomez.

Dr Gomez diagnosed Post Traumatic Stress Syndrome, which he assumed was the result of the 'abuse' Joss had suffered whilst in our care, and he prescribed Risperdal and Paxil. Risperdal is used in the treatment of schizophrenia, bi-polar and autism; Paxil is an anti-depressant used to treat depression, obsessive compulsive disorder, anxiety and Post Traumatic Stress Disorder. One of the major side effects of Paxil is stated to be thoughts of suicide, especially in patients aged under twenty-four.

It seemed that none of these US 'experts' were ever going to accept the diagnosis of ADD.

The Proctors presented their version of the facts to Dr Gomez and he concluded that the allegations of abuse were legitimate. He did this without ever speaking to me or anyone else who would have an appropriate input, and without reviewing any medical records from the UK.

I hope by now you will forgive me for saying that, after everything that had transpired so far, I really did begin to consider – more than consider, if I'm honest – that there was some sort of conspiracy against me and Edward. I was teetering on the brink of actually believing that all of these people, these total strangers, who had never known me or anything about me or my life, were plotting to send me completely mad, to make me lose my mind, to let go of my sanity. I really did begin to think such things.

This was now far more than a custody case. It was now a rescue mission for me to save my children.

Edward and I talked it through for ages, considered the idea over and over, and finally decided to go to the British press. We started making calls. The *Daily Mail* weren't interested – they said they had printed too many stories of a similar nature in recent months. We tried Max Clifford but didn't even get a reply. The *Daily Express*, however, were interested and I made contact with a sympathetic reporter. I began to relate the saga and we discussed one of the allegations made in the recently received document, which was that I had frequently been called in to the boys' school because the staff were observing signs of abuse – apparently, I had not bothered to turn up to the requested meetings! This was, thankfully, something I could easily disprove and the reporter contacted the headmaster at the school, who – naturally – confirmed that this had never been the case and that they had never had any concerns about abuse or about the condition of the boys.

The reporter then called JP's lawyer to relate this conversation and to confront him with the lie, and the reply came down the phone line, *"Oh, well, if you throw enough mud some of it will stick."* These are the words of a legal professional, if you can believe that.

A firm of lawyers in Chicago sent a letter on behalf of JP to the *Daily Express*, basically telling them that they would be on very unsafe ground if they were to consider publishing anything about the case. I quote: *"Be clearly advised that Mr Proctor will take all necessary legal steps to prevent your newspaper's actions from interfering with the welfare of his boys, and will seek all the damages that US law will allow (including punitive damages) if your newspaper proceeds notwithstanding."*

Regrettably, nothing came of this story and I eventually had to drop it.

I had heard of Reunite, the charity set up to help in recovering abducted children: they told me there was no hope of them helping since my case had already been tried and so *"the horse had already bolted".*

A production company called 20/20 who had weekly documentary programmes on Channel 4 TV were working on a feature about child abduction and they contacted Reunite: I was put in touch with them and was very happy to give them my story. They did say they would need to speak to the other party as well – I began to wonder if it might be possible to get the boys back through such publicity. Surely this would not be the action of someone who was, in fact, guilty of the things of which I was accused? I was innocent and had become the victim of the most appalling miscarriage of justice, and I thought – hoped – these people might just be the ones to help me. I gave them Michael Bolton's contact details and someone from 20/20 rang him. Bolton's office hung up on the call and later I received a threatening legal letter accusing Edward and me of trying to exploit the children through involving the media.

On the sixteenth of March, 2000, a letter was sent from JP's lawyer to ours, David Waters, and, as with most of the correspondence around this case by so-called professionals, it paints a picture of an ultimately all-round upstanding good-guy father figure who is desperate to protect his children from the terrible machinations of their evil mother. That's me.

The letter is basically telling Waters to get us to stop trying to involve the media: the reason given is that the boys had had further evaluations and 'extensive counselling' with school district officials and the findings were that Joss had been diagnosed with Post Traumatic Stress Syndrome which was obviously caused by the 'abuse' he suffered when living with us in the UK, that he was suffering 'flashbacks' relating to this abuse, and that we were *"forcing Mr Proctor to take action to protect his children from further beatings and brutality"*. Referring to our attempts to involve the press, the letter says *". . . this new form of exploitation of the children will, without a doubt, cause further severe damage to the boys and prolong their recovery by making their victimization, suffering, disabilities, medical conditions, humiliation and disgrace the subject of international publicity and ceaseless ridicule by their peers."*

It also announces that we would be *"denied further contact until approval by Dr McKay"*, who would be updating her report. The same Dr McKay whose previous report had started this ball rolling, had made this alienation between me and my children actually legal. The very professional who had managed to compile such a report with such adamant conclusions – without ever speaking a single word to me, to Edward, without gleaning any background medical evidence, without any contact with the UK where the boys had lived for most of their lives.

It advised us, in no uncertain terms, that, should we not put a stop to all efforts with the press, *". . . Mr P will enjoin the publication, the invasion of right of privacy, the false light and the defamation, then he will sue the Roches, every accomplice, 20/20 and every other publisher and republisher for the extreme damages they will cause to Joss, Michael and JP III, his wife and himself."*

In the whole two pages, the one sentence that jumps out at me the most is this:

"The most important fact, however, is that the well-being of the boys is in serious jeopardy."

Oh, how true – they were, indeed, in serious jeopardy. But the danger was not emanating from *this* side of the Atlantic. Most definitely not. The danger was their own father – the very person this crazy legal nightmare was declaring to be the boys' protector and saviour.

I was still determined to fight this and I was going to try anything and everything humanly possible. My next lead came to me by pure accident. A girlfriend was telling me that the same thing had happened to a lady called Catherine Meyer when she sent her two sons on a holiday visit to Germany. She is married to Sir Christopher Meyer, the British Ambassador to the US at that time, and the case became very high-profile with numerous magazine articles covering the story.

I found out where to contact Catherine Meyer and I sat and wrote her a letter, telling her of my own plight and basically asking if she could help in any way. A reply came, written by a friend of hers, a lady called Sheelagh Taylor, who I then had a lengthy telephone conversation with – oh, what relief I felt, just to be speaking to someone who actually understood what had happened, and what I was going through.

Sheelagh told me about Catherine's book, *They Are My Children Too*, and I couldn't wait to get hold of a copy. As our conversation came to an end, Sheelagh told me to research Parental Alienation – she added that there wasn't much information available on the internet just yet, but that it was becoming more of a topic of interest.

Catherine Meyer says:

"The child has already been traumatised by the loss of one parent; his greatest fear becomes that he will lose the other parent. This fear itself then becomes an obstacle to resolving the situation, since it is central to what is known as Parental Alienation Syndrome (PAS).

Studies of PAS have established the severity of psychological damage done to abducted children who are suddenly separated from a parent. The studies have also shown how susceptible the child is to being systematically alienated by the abductor parent from the victim parent.

. . . for fear of losing the abducting parent as well, the child will not only be eager to please but ready to believe allegations that it has been abandoned by the victim parent. This is fertile ground for systematic indoctrination by the abducting parent and/or a professional psychologist. Since, under some judicial systems, children – sometimes as young as three – may be required to appear in court, it becomes of paramount importance to abducting parents that their children say 'the right thing' to judges. This puts an even higher premium on placing psychological pressure on abducted children."

(They Are My Children Too, Catherine Meyer © 1999 by Catherine Meyer, published by Public Affairs ™ USA)

Sitting at my computer, I just couldn't hit the keys quickly enough to see what material there was on the subject of Parental Alienation. Sheelagh was right, in that there were very few books or papers written, but one name came up time and time again. Richard Gardner. I ordered his most recent book and also one called *Divorce Casualties – Protecting Yourself from Parental Alienation* by Douglas Darnall. These books could only be obtained from the States and they weren't available in any book shops in the UK. Knowledge is power! It was these books that would give me the details and the information I so desperately needed in order to discover what was really going on. They would teach me about just how JP had, as I had put it, 'got into their minds'.

That summer I travelled down to my sister's place in the South of France, and I spent all my time lying by the pool, reading my new books. I was totally engrossed in the pages as each one unfolded more and more of what I needed to understand, the ammunition I needed in order to fight this battle properly. I scribbled reams of notes, I couldn't be distracted from my studies until I was finished. I was going to prove what JP had done to my children and nothing was going to stop me.

Chapter eleven

what is Parental Alienation Syndrome?

It was Richard Gardner MD, clinical professor of child psychiatry at the College of Physicians and Surgeons, Columbia University, who, in 1985, introduced the term Parental Alienation Syndrome (PAS) into the arena of child custody litigation.

Richard Gardner is recognised as one of the leading innovators in his field, he is certified by the American Board of Psychiatry and Neurology and is a Life Fellow of the American Psychiatric Association and a Fellow of the American Academy of Child and Adolescent Psychiatry and of the American Academy of Psychoanalysis. He is listed in *Who's Who in America* and also in *Who's Who in the World.*

It would be difficult, if not impossible, to find someone more able or better qualified to impart information on PAS. Gardner's books are regarded as the definitive works on the subject.

He identified eight symptoms of PAS in children, as follows:

1. The campaign of denigration
2. Weak, frivolous and absurd rationalisations for the deprecation
3. Lack of ambivalence
4. The 'independent-thinker' phenomenon

5. Reflexive support of the alienating parent in the parental conflict
6. Absence of guilt over cruelty to and/or exploitation of the alienated parent
7. Presence of borrowed scenarios
8. Spread of the animosity to the extended family of the alienated parent

I made it my business to research the subject of PAS as much as humanly possible, and I have read Dr Gardner's books in detail. The more I read, the more I realised that my children were, in truth and whether I liked it or not, victims of PAS.

On the first point of the campaign of denigration, Dr Gardner says: *"It is important that the reader appreciate that the campaign of denigration has two components: the alienating parent's indoctrination and the child's own contributions. As mentioned, it is this combination that warrants the PAS diagnosis. Often, the child's contributions will piggyback on the parent's indoctrinations and provide elaborations not even mentioned by the programming parent. In many cases the elaborations are ludicrous, and even preposterous, thereby providing the clue to their speciousness."*

Asking the question as to whether the child's campaign of denigration is conscious or unconscious, Gardner advises *". . . what may have begun as a conscious and deliberate fabrication may ultimately end up as a delusion in which the child actually believes that the vilified parent is abhorrent, because the delusional material has become fixed in the child's brain circuitry. This is a common progression."*

In his summation of the effects of PAS on a child, Gardner states *"PAS children develop problems in reality testing. They are programmed to believe things that do not coincide with their observations and experiences. This can produce confusion, feelings of self-doubt, low self-worth, distrust of those who tell them things differently from the programmer, and, in extreme cases, psychotic breaks with reality. Impaired reality testing is one of the hallmarks of psychosis. Frequent mention has been made of the paranoid delusional system that is often induced in PAS children, a delusional system that may last for years, if not throughout the course of the child's life.*

PAS children are taught to be psychopathic. They are encouraged to act out their hostility with guiltless disregard for the effects of their behaviour on the targeted parent. When the campaign of denigration spreads to the vilified parent's extended family, PAS children lose a significant portion of their family support system. This cannot but produce feelings of insecurity and loneliness.

Although the PAS child overtly gloats over the rejection of the despised parent, somewhere deep down there is usually a feeling of great loss. After all, a loved and cherished person has now been removed entirely from the child's life. Such loss can produce feelings of depression without the freedom to express what the child is depressed about. These problems can all interfere with school adjustment, interpersonal relationships and sibling relationships, and can cause a wide variety of other psychological problems."

Gardner defined PAS as *"the programming of a child by one parent to denigrate the other."*

Douglas Darnall, PhD, at the time of publishing his book *Divorce Casualties* in 1998, was a licensed psychologist and CEO of PsyCare, an outpatient psychology centre in Youngstown, Ohio, where he taught workshops on parental alienation syndrome and divorce to mental health care professionals.

Darnall says *"Parental alienation is long overdue as a term and a concept to be understood by all divorcing parents and the professionals involved. Children have a right to a loving relationship with both parents . . ."* At the time of writing, Darnall had spent fourteen years working as a psychologist specialising in custody litigation, with over six hundred families. In his chapter on

'How Parents Alienate', he says *"Obsessed alienators are typically more blatant in their comments and actions against the targeted parent . . . Whatever motivates the alienator, the results are almost always the same. The alienating parent strives to strengthen the children's psychological dependency on himself while sacrificing the children's relationship with the other parent. This dependency is an interesting phenomenon. The children are taught to not trust their own perceptions and feelings about the other parent and, instead, are told to trust and believe in what the alienating parent says about the targeted parent. Whatever the children think about the other parent, the alienating parent will somehow subvert the beliefs and replace them with their own. Over time, the alienating parent succeeds in having their children become their parrots. They no longer have their own opinions or beliefs. When this happens, the obsessed alienator is ecstatic and triumphant. You can imagine what this does to the children's self-esteem and sense of individuality."*

(The Parental Alienation Syndrome, Second Edition, Richard A. Gardner, MD © 1992, 1998 by Creative Therapeutics Inc., New Jersey)
(Divorce Casualties: Protecting Your Children from Parental Alienation, Douglas Darnall, PhD © Douglas Darnall 1998, published by Taylor Publishing Company, Dallas, Texas)

Where does PAS come from?

In our lives we have all met the aggrieved thirty-something mother, anxious and alone with her young child. Her husband (or partner) – the man she loved and believed in, the man with whom she was certain she was to spend her entire future, has left her. Not only left, but he has started a whole new life with someone else – a life he must have been planning for some time, while she carried on, unaware of the pain and turmoil ahead. And now she faces an uncertain future, afraid and deeply hurt, emotionally scarred, her mind racing to work out what went wrong, to find an answer to the question 'how could he do this to his wife and child?'

But answers don't come. The mother struggles through each day, clinging to a handful of friends, those who have 'taken her side' as opposed to those friends *of theirs* with whom she has cut off all contact because they are still seeing him. Her world has suddenly diminished, her lifestyle has had to change – no way can she afford the mortgage on her own, running a car is no longer taken for granted but has become a luxury she can barely afford, she can't go out because she can't afford to but also she feels so worthless and unattractive, she feels safer staying home, curled up on the settee with the bottle of wine she knows she shouldn't buy but it helps her through the lonely evenings while she imagines him in his new, happy life.

This mother does not *intend* to cause any damage to the relationship her child has with his father, and she certainly would never *intentionally* cause any damage to her child, but – without even realising what is happening – she is *inadvertently* causing PAS to occur.

A simple and innocent telephone call from a well-meaning close friend, asking *"How are you, do you need anything, is there anything I can do to help?"* Relieved to have someone to listen, a sympathetic ear, the mother pours out the latest episodes of the break-up; she is so wrapped up in her own grief and loss, she cannot hear herself and what she is saying. She calls her ex's new partner 'that cheap tart' and describes him as 'the selfish evil bastard' and generally paints her picture of a wronged woman abandoned with her child, and a totally guilty and uncaring ex. She asks her friend *"How does he think little Johnny is coping with this? How could he do this to his own flesh and blood? He doesn't even care that we aren't managing financially and I bet that tart of his isn't doing without food or clothes . . ."* and so it goes.

The only thing this woman is guilty of is being hurt and needing to off-load. What she is actually doing is this. The child hears all of her complaints and criticisms, realises that mum is hurt and that dad and this other woman have caused that. This child is already suffering the loss of his father, who has left the family home and who the child now sees once a fortnight and, even then, only for a short while. So, the child knows he must not risk losing the other parent as well, at any cost, and so goes to great lengths to ensure this doesn't happen. The child takes on board what mum is saying about dad and his new partner and this becomes the child's reality. Dad becomes the person who has abandoned them, left them unable to cope and made mum so upset and sad all the time.

This child is now being programmed – *albeit unintentionally* – to turn against his father, to be alienated from him.

The other side of the coin . . .

Or, far worse than this, PAS can be completely intentional, calculated, engineered – the act of someone whose aim, for whatever reasons, is to cut off all contact, to destroy beyond repair all physical, mental and emotional relationship between the child and the other parent.

The reasons for doing this can be:

Financial – the absconding partner has left the mother or father of the child in an unstable financial situation; the breadwinner has gone, money was not a problem until now, their lifestyle had always been more than ample, nice home, quality cars, foreign holidays . . . and so on. Now we are talking about claiming benefits, trying to find a job, childcare, somewhere to live, having to rely on family and friends . . . so much loss.

Revenge – someone who is so hurt and feels rejected, worthless, abandoned, unattractive . . . whose partner has gone to start a new life with someone else – the future they should be sharing with *you*, the lifestyle *you* deserve, the security and bright future you thought *you* had with them – all gone, nothing left. Revenge is a huge driving force and can cause someone to turn a child against the absent parent purely because it will hurt that person and 'this is the only way I can get at you – through our child'.

Whatever the reasoning and whether it is unintentional or not, all parents with children who separate *must* be aware of the child's right to have a good relationship with *both* parents, and that this is a great part of the child's healthy development.

PAS – the deadly force to be reckoned with.

On the twenty-seventh of August, 2004, Dr Rick Lohstroh drove his SUV to his ex-wife's home to collect their two little boys for a regular visitation. He pulled up outside the house and waited. A few minutes later, he was dead. Shot in the back of the head by his ten-year-old son.

Dr Lohstroh and his ex-wife both had successful careers in the medical field in Galveston, Texas, they had a lovely home and two healthy children. But their marriage was far from happy: there was constant domestic violence and the police had been called to their home on several occasions. After his death, Mrs Lohstroh blamed all of this on him, but statements from friends and neighbours clearly indicate that she had been the aggressor.

The couple went through an acrimonious divorce and custody battle, which ended in Dr Lohstroh having equal parenting rights to the children. Then, having been thwarted in her various machinations, the enraged and vengeful Mrs Lohstroh resorted to even more excessive measures. She had already been exhibiting a very aggressive and manipulative style of Parental Alienation, including hurling accusations at the boys' father of physical and sexual abuse – all of which were proven to be false.

Her determination to be avenged knew no bounds, and on this last visitation, she put her gun into the hands of her little boy and told him to go and shoot daddy in the back.

According to the records of this case, the boy got into the back seat, shot his father once, and returned to the house, only to be sent back to the car to continue shooting. The little boy emptied the entire cartridge into his father.

At the trial in 2006, the boy claimed that his father had abused him, but he was sentenced to ten years in the custody of the Texas Youth Commission. After serving five years, the conviction was reversed and he was released into the care of his maternal grandmother.

Some evidence had not been allowed at the trial, evidence which illustrated that the boy had believed he was defending himself and his little brother. The boy's attorney said *"Mum is, and always has been, a suspect."*

Chapter twelve

the battle continues . . .

One evening, sitting in the living-room, there was a loud knock at the front door. We weren't expecting anyone and it wasn't a visitor, it was a delivery of a package that we had to sign for. Once opened, this package revealed its hellish contents – a document listing the most awful allegations against us, and every one a tissue of lies and manipulation. To add insult to injury, there was a demand for punitive damages and monies to be paid to JP. Was there no end to this man's evil?

The battle, it seemed, had only just begun.

The document was an official, legal petition issued from the Thirteenth Judicial District Court in the County of Sandoval, State of New Mexico, and it was dated the third of May, 2000.

It had the grandiose title of *First Amended Verified Petition for Emergency Protective Order, Temporary Restraining Order, Permanent Injunction, Motion to Modify Divorce Decree and for Damages.*

It includes the totally incorrect entry: *"This matter received an all day hearing on January 28 1999 . . ."* when, in fact, the hearing had been held on the twenty-eighth of January, 2000. The attacks on me personally, and on Edward, were notable:

"Pamela Roche experienced a change of circumstance, which placed the children at risk. She made imprudent financial decisions, failed to seek employment and eventually moved to England for assistance from her family and to live in a home provided to her by her immediate family."

So where did he expect me to be living, when the sum of money he had legally committed to pay to me in order for me to buy a house in England where I would live with the boys, had never materialised? We had both signed an *Agreement Incident to Divorce*, the purpose of which was:

"to settle forever and completely the rights of the parties as between themselves and their heirs and assigns, in and to all property, including assets, debts, and obligations . . ."

and Section 3.04 of this Agreement states:

"Husband agrees to make a down payment not exceeding $80,000 upon a house of Wife's choice, said down payment not exceeding $80,000 to be made by Husband on or before December 31, 1991. This house shall be the property of Wife . . ."

This sum of money was never paid, not one penny of it.

This same Agreement included provision for the children, as follows:

"Support of Children 6.01 Cash Payments. The parties agree that Husband shall pay to Wife child support in the amount of $5,000 per month, with the first payment being due and payable on the 10th day of the month following the month in which judgment is rendered herein, and a like payment being due and payable on the same day of each month

thereafter until the date any child reaches the age of 21 or is otherwise emancipated. Wife shall apply these funds for the support, education and welfare of the children. If Wife should remarry, the child support is reduced to $3,000 per month as adjusted in 6.05."

To continue with the character assassination . . .

"From approximately 1993 to 1995, Respondent lived with Edward Roche under the same roof with the children without being married. This exposed the children to, and approved of immorality substandard family values by example. During such times, the treatment of the children deteriorated and the children became subject to physical and emotional abuse from Pamela Roche's live-in."

Perhaps in the UK in this period, we were slightly more open-minded about couples co-habiting than they obviously were in New Mexico. And, as to the 'abuse' – where is the proof of any of this? There is none. And let us remind ourselves that, during this time, the boys both attended school, mixed with friends and neighbours, had medical checks, enjoyed sports and social activities . . . surely someone in all of this would have noticed if even a tiny part of this were true?

Remember, also, that Joss had recently been seen regularly by Poole Hospital, clinics and senior medical practitioners. The abuse described in this document could not possibly have escaped the attention of such closely monitored medical investigations.

"On information and belief, Pamela Roche is a battered wife and has developed the battered wife's syndrome and is unable to protect or supervise the children. There is obvious lack of medical care for the children."

Information? What information, exactly, could that be? Again, there is none because this is totally untrue. People notice when one is 'battered' – family, friends, neighbours, medical practitioners, education professionals . . . all sorts of people. But there was nothing *to notice*.

Lack of medical care? What about Joss' medical records? The entire document was a bad joke.

But then the unassailable Dr McKay rears her head once more with a real gem:

> *"The emotional problems will, in the opinion of Dr McKay necessitate at least eight years of regular treatment. Based on the present costs of such treatment, the therapy will cost at least $1,500.00 each month for at least 8 years. The costs of the home schooling are valued at at least $365.00 per month plus school supplies and facilities. There will be other costs associated with remediating the effects of the abuse including Petitioner's lost time from their usual activities, expenses associated with the treatments, medication, associated examinations and medical expenses, corrective medical and dental treatment, schooling expenses, activity expenses, home care expenses, the value of the assistance of others in caring for Joss during this period and such other costs and expenses as may be determined."*

Can anyone believe that the total being demanded was – give or take – exactly the amount owed to me by JP in unpaid child maintenance. An amazing coincidence?

There were vivid descriptions of the alleged abuse, including *"whippings with belt buckles"*, *"being punched in the face"* and *"being shoved against walls"*. I realise I am repeating myself, but such actions by an adult against a child would – without a doubt – leave marks which would be noticed by others. But there were never any such marks, because none of this ever took place.

Section 9A of this ridiculous document states that:

"Doctor McKay after examining the children was compelled to report the abuse to the children to the New Mexico Child Protective Service Department as required by the New Mexico Abuse and Neglect act 32A-1-1 et seq. NMSA 1978."

And she did this without once making any enquiry as to medical background, family background, educational background, without speaking to one single person in the UK who could submit proven factual information about the boys, without ever once consulting me or my family . . . so clever is this woman, she obviously rises above such basic procedures.

And it was she, and she alone, who set this ball rolling, put this dreadful sequence of events into motion, and it was she alone whose unfounded, inept, inaccurate and totally biased report ensured that I would lose my children.

I trust she is very proud of her work.

In my conversations with the charity Reunite[3], they had given me a telephone number for a lawyer in the States called Linda Shay-Gardner, who was recommended by them as a very good Hague Convention lawyer. In fact, they included her name in their promotional brochure. I was by now wishing the Lord Chancellor's office had put us on to her instead of Mr Waters – who had been so wrong to be confident and casual about the outcome of that awful hearing. I did think, however, perhaps even she wouldn't have been able to exert any influence, given the boys' terrible behaviour in the judge's chambers . . .

But that's history now, and I needed to move on. I called Linda and related my story to her, including the dreadful

---

3   *Reunite recorded 269 abduction cases handled by their advice line between January and October 2009, involving a total of 386 children. Their web site states there was a 164% increase in abduction cases from 1995 to 2010.*

outcome. She was genuinely appalled that this had been allowed to happen and that the boys had not been returned to the UK. She told me that I would have very little chance of winning a custody case in the US – in fact, she said 'practically zero'. I replied that I didn't care, I just knew I had to keep fighting . . . I couldn't give up believing that truth and justice would win in the end. I felt my position was now much stronger, given my research into PAS, and I just knew I had to rescue my boys, whatever it was going to take.

Linda checked her list of contacts and gave me a number for a young lawyer in Albuquerque, although she did add that she had only worked with him on the one occasion. This was my first introduction to Michael Keene.

I thought it would be wise to make contact with Michael Keene initially by telephone: you can, I believe, get a much better impression of someone when you can hear each other's voices, rather than merely exchanging minimal words on a computer screen or in a formal letter. And this was way too important for me to make a decision unless I had some sense of what this man was all about.

We spoke, and I explained as much as it is possible to divulge in a first conversation about something so huge and so complex, so overwhelming. Michael Keene agreed to take the case on. When I asked him if he had any experience of PAS cases, he replied that he didn't but that that was something for the psychologists to look into. I found this refreshingly honest and professional. I liked this man and so did Edward. We felt confident that we wanted him working for us.

His fees were two hundred and fifty dollars an hour and we gladly paid an up-front retainer of ten thousand dollars, then we arranged to meet him when we were next flying to the States. He was a young man, around thirty, and he was an Associate of the David Crane law firm in Albuquerque.

Michael talked us through the legal process, explained who would be involved and basically how matters would proceed. That was in September 2000.

Chapter thirteen

moving on

Never one to stay too long in one place, in September 2000
JP moved his family to a tiny place – not even a town – called
Abiquiu, which is in an extremely isolated area of New Mexico,
very close to the Colorado border.

Joss was moved to the Espanola Middle School where he
was accompanied by a full-time aide whose job was to help
him modify his anti-social behaviour.

I can't explain how this felt, knowing my son was suffering,
having to deal with being uprooted and moved around – this
time to a middle-of-nowhere place – having to deal with a
strange school, new people, bearing the slur of being regarded
as anti-social, and feeling the humiliation of needing an aide,
to be constantly on heavy medication (and what about possible
side-effects?) which must be affecting how he felt, thought,
acted . . . to be the mother of such a child and to be forcibly
kept from doing anything to help him – was the worst kind
of pain.

Chapter fourteen

the Guardian

That July, a man named Jeffrey Hoffmann was appointed Guardian Ad Litem (GAL) which meant he would act as lawyer for the boys. On the thirtieth of August, 2000, Hoffmann sent a letter to Michael Bolton, JP's lawyer, and to Michael Keene, outlining his fees and how these would be dispersed, and also requesting copies of all pleadings filed in this case. He also asked Michael Keene to let him know when I would be in Albuquerque so that we could arrange to meet, at the same time asking Bolton about arranging one meeting with JP and a separate meeting with the children.

We met Hoffmann in September, on the same trip to the States as our meeting with Michael Keene. A man in his early fifties, he struck us immediately as being completely disinterested in the case and he was incredibly dismissive towards us. He had already, it was obvious, formed his own opinions and he made it clear that he had no time for us and was simply going through the motions.

Sitting in his office, I was trying to show him photos of the boys in England, letters from friends, neighbours, the school, all portraying the normal, happy life the boys had led with us – a life that was light years away from the horrible picture being painted so cleverly by JP and those around him.

But Hoffmann showed not a flicker of interest whatsoever in any of this and it was clearly a waste of time trying to get him to take on board any of the evidence we were putting before him.

Having the position of GAL was very important and very serious. It meant that this man's opinion was going to carry a lot of weight. This was not looking good.

Chapter fifteen

testing times

In August 2000, the Thirteenth Judicial District Court of Sandoval, New Mexico, ordered a psychological evaluation to be carried out on the boys, the Proctors, Edward and myself.

Dr Simon Rowe was the 706 psychological expert appointed by this court for such evaluations. We met with him at his office, located in the student sector of Albuquerque – the place was a rather modest and inconspicuous family home built of wood.

Dr Rowe was quite short in stature, but it soon became clear that he made up for this in his pompous and self-opinionated attitude.

The first few days were taken up with the personality tests: *Minnesota Multi Phasic Personality Inventory* (MMPI 2) is one of the most frequently applied testing methods in mental health, and is used by trained professionals to assist in identifying personality structure and psychopathy. The clinical scales are designed to measure common diagnoses: Scale 1 measures a person's perception and pre-occupation with their health and health issues; Scale 2 measures a person's depression symptoms levels; Scale 3 measures the emotionality of a person; Scale 4 measures a person's need for control or rebellion against control; Scale 5 measures the stereotype of a person and how they compare; Scale 6 measures a person's ability/inability to trust; Scale 7 measures a person's anxiety levels and tendencies; Scale 8 measures a person's unusual/off cognitive, perceptual and emotional experiences; Scale 9 measures a person's energy and Scale 0 measures whether people enjoy, and are comfortable around, other people.

We had a total of five hundred and sixty-seven statements to which we had to respond, which took almost a full day. For information, I list a few examples; the answers had to be either Yes, No or Sometimes.

I like mechanic magazines
I would like to work in a library
There seems to be a lump in my throat most of the time
Once in a while I think of things too bad to talk about
I sure get a raw deal out of life
No-one seems to understand me
I would like to be a singer
My hands and feet are usually warm enough

Then there was the Thematic Apperception Test (TAT). For this we had to respond to cards showing ambiguous images of different situations, and we were asked to create a story about each image – this allows the person being tested to project their own feelings into the pictures, rather than having to express them personally. Our responses provide information relating to our views of self, the world and interpersonal relationships.

When we had completed this, we met with Dr Rowe individually and we each gave our own account of events leading up to this point. We showed him the photos and letters from the school, from friends and the medical records from the UK. This was all the 'evidence' we had – it's strange, but, unless you can foresee such catastrophic events in your life, you are not really prepared for having to try to convince people that you are in the right. You don't, for example, think to take a thousand photos of every time your children smile or laugh, you don't think to constantly get the people in your life to write and sign statements to support the fact that you are a good person, you simply don't ever think there would be a need for this kind of day-by-day testimonial.

We now know there can be such a need.

I had no option but to pray that this man, the latest in a succession of 'professionals' involved along the way since this nightmare began, would see the reality of the situation, would realise what the truth was, and would be left with no alternative but to have my children returned to me.

The following day, we were to meet with the boys and the GAL, Hoffmann. I had made my point that, under no circumstances, did I want the Proctors to be present. When we arrived, imagine my horror to see the Proctors' car outside and, standing in the front doorway, was Tess Proctor on her mobile phone! She didn't see us and so we drove round the back of the building until she had gone. I wasn't going to cross paths with her just now.

I couldn't help myself: I stormed into the building and demanded to know why they had been allowed to be there. It would make the boys think they needed to be protected from us. Rowe tried to make light of it, saying *"It's OK, they are only in the back room."* They had even brought along a friend of theirs – this turned out to be another of JP's cronies, a chap called Skip Winters: the boys called him Uncle Skip. How utterly unprofessional of Rowe, and – worse than that – he had lied to us, which illustrated how very much he was *not* on our side.

What came next was worse than my very darkest fears. We were supposed to be seeing the boys which, of course, filled me with so many emotions – I so desperately wanted to see them, of course I did – in the past ten months I had not seen or spoken to the boys, apart from the one telephone conversation in August . . . but, remembering their demeanour in that courtroom, this desperate desire was also filled with trepidation – how would they be? Would they be pleased to see me? Or would they be in the same state as last time we saw them? The anticipation was physically sickening and my head felt it was about to explode.

The sounds coming from that back room were unbelievable – screaming, wailing, retching noises from the boys and this went on and on, sounds of general hysteria. It took twenty minutes before they came out to see us.

What we actually experienced was horrific, unreal. For the first thirty minutes of the contact, my boys behaved as if they were possessed – that's the only way to describe it. They shouted, they swore, they screamed – and we could do nothing. They actually had to be restrained when it was apparent they were going to physically attack Edward and me. Their shouting and ranting formed a barrage of vile hatred, a foul-mouthed abusive attack on us both – including, however unbelievable this was, accusations of sexual abuse by Edward. The poor man was devastated. All he had ever done was provide for them, give them a loving home and care for them. He had been a real father to them.

The torrent of anger and hatred included calling us names such as 'fucking bitch', 'pig'; screaming at Edward that he had sexually abused them and telling him he belonged 'in the state penitentiary'. Joss had to be taken out of the room, as he was beside himself with anger. Michael continued with the attack: *"Why did you come here? Why can't you just leave us alone? Why don't you just release me? You don't care about us! You called me ignorant! You took my childhood away from me!"*

When the boys had been at home, they had been very fond

of their baby sister, Daniella: now, it seemed, their hatred even applied to her. *"Why don't you leave us alone and just look after that baby?"* Michael called me 'Pam' and told me that Tess was now their real mother. I have to say, this hurt more than everything else.

Michael shouted at us that we used to go to the pub, leaving him and Joss alone in the house with the baby. Although completely ludicrous, I could see he seemed to actually believe what he was saying. He shouted that he had never had tennis lessons, never went for walks with dog by the river . . . all rubbish, but he really seemed convinced he was telling the truth.

We were in shock, absolutely speechless, at this overwhelming rage, this pure hatred towards us. The boys had had nothing but a happy life with us in England and there was no earthly reason, no sensible explanation for this hellish behaviour.

All I knew was, their father was at the root of it all.

It's just one single small word. Sorry. Most of us say it quite readily, easily. Sometimes for no real reason. You bump into a stranger in a shop doorway. Sorry. It takes less than a second. Then you both move on, go your separate ways. No consequences, no big story.

If I could go back in time, there are oh, so many things I would change, but the one thing that has haunted my every waking moment since I realised I was being plunged into a living nightmare, the one tiny word I spoke that told those people who knew nothing about me, about my life, my family, the word that gave them reason to believe I was guilty – how I would change that.

I said sorry.

I spoke the word as a mother who was fighting for her children, trying to get them back, away from their controlling father, away from being used as mere mechanisms to be operated, to perform exactly to his bidding, to have no mind of their own. I spoke the word as a mother whose heart was being torn to pieces as she watched her two babies turn into soulless beings devoid of love, of affection, of life itself. I spoke the word because it was all I could say to express how utterly, completely sorry I was that my sons were having to live through this madness, having to experience evil such as I had never thought possible. I said sorry because there were no other words, I said sorry because I was being bullied, pushed, provoked, by a total stranger who had already made up his mind that I was guilty, when all I wanted to do was reach out and gather my little boys up in my arms, to hold them close and make it all go away. Make it all right.

I said sorry because I was listening to my two boys wailing and crying in another room, listening to them hurling abuse at Edward. Awful, terrible accusations – things you don't ever expect to hear from the mouths of your own children. I said sorry because my children were being restrained and I could not help them.

It was as if the devil himself had his hands around my throat, the ugly molten sinews choking the very life out of me. Inside my head, screaming. So much awful, deathly screaming. Pounding in my ears. For how long, I don't know, but I wanted to cry out, to faint, to run, to escape all of this evil, this madness that threatened to engulf me until I, too, was mad and the world would no longer make any sense at all.

But I did nothing. I sat beside Edward, barely conscious, hearing the dreadful words being hurled at us by my children, the babies I had carried inside me. Words my beautiful boys should not be speaking

I was sorry this was happening, sorry I couldn't stop it, sorry I had been let down by the legal system, sorry I could not protect my own flesh and blood.

And, because I said sorry, they said I must be guilty.

I was not guilty. And neither was Edward. But there we both sat, in the office of Dr Rowe, the psychologist appointed by the court to carry out a psychological evaluation on us both. We had requested that the Proctors would not be present, but there they were, even though Dr Rowe had previously agreed to our request.

We sat, feeling we must have gone to sleep and woken up in a different world, a place where our opinions counted for nothing, where we had no voice, where everything we believed in was trashed, where we were less than human.

I was a prisoner accused of a crime I did not commit and I could do nothing to prove it. My whole being was in shock, disbelief. I looked at the boys. Poor Joss was obviously very ill, and I could tell he was on heavy medication.

Dr Rowe spoke to Michael. *"Michael, tell me what Edward made you do."* Then I heard Michael's voice in reply, *"He told me to take my clothes off and then he said walk round the bed and he put his penis in my bottom."* No words can describe the horror of hearing your child speak such lies, things they had been made to say, indoctrinated by someone so evil they could corrupt their own innocent children in the interests of self and money.

My brain was desperately trying to take in what must have been going on. My ex-husband – father of my children – who I had married and shared a life with, had brainwashed our boys to such an extent they seemed to believe the vile accusations they were repeating. If anyone will rot in hell, surely it will be him. Please, God, save us all.

I managed to speak. I asked Dr Rowe if he had ever seen children so alienated. He replied, almost glibly, that he had seen worse. Then he asked me what I thought Michael wanted me to say.

What else could I say. So I just said *"Sorry."*

With that dreadful time in Rowe's office now over, I reflected on his response to being asked if he had ever seen children so extremely alienated. He'd replied, *"Oh, yes, I have – much worse."*

What could possibly be 'much worse' than what we had just witnessed? Apart from the boys actually attacking, injuring – or even killing – me and Edward, nothing could be 'much worse' than what had taken place. Something was making me focus on this. The boys' behaviour was oppositional in the extreme – excessively dramatic, completely shocking. I also realised it ticked a lot of the boxes listed in Gardner's book on PAS, in the descriptions of how alienated children behave. I had studied sufficiently by now to realise what was happening and also to realise that I would be up against people who would have no knowledge of PAS and who would not be particularly open to any such suggestion, especially from a non-professional.

I decided to try to speak to Rowe and I heard myself telling him what I had learned about the early signs of PAS, which I hadn't been able to recognise at the time but now I felt qualified to at least put this forward. To illustrate my point, I recounted the incident that took place when JP handed the boys back to me once, following a visit with him. All three of them – Michael, Joss and their father – made this strange sign with their fingers to each other and I asked JP what it was all about. He had replied *"Oh, just boys' talk – things only fathers and sons understand."* It was like a silly little secret pact between them, and mum was obviously not going to be privy to any explanation. The boys returned home with a special sing-song that they would chant together, about the Proctor boys all being together as one. My recent studies of PAS revealed that secret signs, phrases, chants and so on were among the early signs of PAS. The victimised parent is portrayed as someone who doesn't want to have fun, while the alienating parent is the one who understands. Normal disciplinary measures are distorted by fantasies, misrepresentations, exaggerations, delusions and vicious deliberate lies.

Rowe's response to my outpouring proved to me that he wasn't prepared to consider the existence of PAS; in fact, at a later date, he was to confirm this negative attitude in court. He really had no time for the idea that the boys could have been alienated by their father and his cronies.

Once again, I was enveloped in a really bad feeling, ominous, threatening.

We flew back to the UK, unable to shake off the effects on us both from that dreadful experience. We could do nothing now but wait for Rowe's report to turn up. The longer we waited, the more convinced we were that it would definitely not be in our favour. If Rowe had taken on board the possibility that this was, or could be, a case of PAS, he would have produced his report quickly in order to have the boys removed from the custody of the alienating parent. As each day passed, I felt our hopes diminish.

Chapter sixteen

the report

Dr Rowe's report didn't appear until December 2000, almost four months after the evaluations were carried out. It consisted of six pages. We opened it with a mixture of hope and fear.

The report began with a *Brief History* – all what you would expect, factual information giving names, dates, events and so on. We did expect to see a full report from all of the tests we took, but instead we read:

> *"a great deal of information was collected to make recommendations for this family. However, it is neither useful nor necessary for each of the adults to have their full evaluations described in this report. This is especially true in a case such as this, in which there is considerable anger and disagreement. In such cases, there is the additional risk that the parties will use the information to continue their battles and thereby cause future harm to the children."*

This made sense, and Rowe did offer *"the extensive data collected about each adult is available and I am open to reviewing each person's own test results, in detail, during individual consultation."* So we didn't get the feeling he was trying to hide anything, but was simply concentrating on information about the boys, which was what this whole fiasco was about.

> *"Joss, who has been diagnosed and treated for Attention Defect Disorder, is actually suffering from many, more serious psychological difficulties . . . Joss' thinking is highly congruent with the diagnosis of childhood schizophrenia. He has chronic and pervasive problems that interfere with his correct perception of reality. His distortion of reality is frequent enough to cause considerable difficulty maintaining adequate adjustment in most situations, for any extended period. In addition to serious perceptual difficulties, Joss has severe difficulty thinking. He organizes information, correctly or incorrectly perceived, in idiosyncratic and highly illogical ways.*
>
> *In addition to psychotic-level difficulties in thinking and perception, Joss has a grossly inaccurate, negative, and tormented sense of self. He sees himself as damaged and inadequate even in those areas in which he would be viewed positive by others. Since he is excessively insecure about his physical and psychological integrity, when challenged, Joss becomes obsessive, oppositional, and argumentative. Unfortunately, Joss has never received an in-depth psychological evaluation nor has he received psychiatric or psychological treatment appropriate for his serious difficulties."*

The report went on to describe Joss' very negative feelings towards Edward, and fear of him – he was afraid of retaliation for having told about the physical and sexual abuse that was supposed to have taken place.

> *"While Joss is very angry with his mother, Mrs Roche, his*

negative feelings for her are mixed with feelings of tenderness, concern and longing. He wants to have contact with Mrs Roche but is fearful that it would necessitate contact with Mr Roche."

This was very difficult for me to read. To see, in black and white, that Joss was 'longing' to see me. And, again, there was nothing I could say or do to be with him, be with my children.

About Michael, the report said:

". . . He becomes apprehensive and anxious when he has emotions or impulses which do not match parental and conventional expectations. It is as if Michael is heavily invested in being a 'good boy' even when it means distorting his own experiences and feelings. He believes that he must deny and distort his unacceptable or negative feelings if he is to be loveable or even acceptable.

While Michael's description of physical abuse is less extensive than Joss' . . . Michael does not report the extensive sexual abuse by Mr Roche that Joss does . . ."

This was a lie: without Joss in the room, Michael described in detail what Edward was supposed to have done to him. It was all so obviously coached . . .

The *Findings* of the report included:

"1. Joss and Michael are so angry with and fearful of Mrs and Mr Roche that it would seriously harm the children to be in their custody."

Short, sharp and to the point. Just like being stabbed.

But further reading served to raise my hopes in one instant and, before I could blink an eye, dash them again without mercy. I found myself alternately agreeing with what I read, and then recoiling from the words as if they were physically wounding me.

> "Mr and Mrs Proctor have, in mostly indirect and unconscious ways, contributed to the children's negative reactions to Mr and Mrs Roche . . .
>
> Joss' extensive complaints of sexual abuse were not confirmed. It is difficult to tell how many, if any, of the explicit accounts are true . . . The accounts of sexual misconduct against the children have not been substantiated."

So many questions arise from reading this report. How can it be said that a child is afraid of reprisals for telling about something they claim happened, and then later say these claims can't be substantiated? If the boys have been in such a bad way for so long, and they have by now lived with JP and Tess for a year, why has nothing been done to get them help, treatment? Why is no-one asking the Proctors if they consider it good parenting to ignore such drastic mental health issues for a whole year? The report notes the *"hostile, aggressive interactions with Mr Roche"* as the main cause of the alienation against myself and Edward, and then goes on to say the reasons for these interactions, as claimed, cannot be proven.

And then came the *Recommendations:*

> 1. The children cannot return to the custody of Mrs Roche. They should be in the custody of Mr Proctor.
> 2. In spite of the difficulties of distance and expense, it is imperative that the relationship between the children and Mrs Roche be rehabilitated. It is in the children's best interest that the highest economic priority be given to arranging for at least twice yearly visits between the children and Mrs Roche. As economic factors allow,

more visits should be arranged. The visits should be coordinated by the Guardian Ad Litem so that the children feel protected. Mrs Roche and the children have time together without the presence of the Proctors, and some time is reserved for therapy sessions for Mrs Roche and the children.

3. *Once the relationship between Mrs Roche and the children has been rehabilitated, other, more extended forms of visitation, should be considered.*

4. *Joss must have appropriate psychological treatment. The seriousness of his condition and the length of time left untreated may eventually necessitate a protracted, psychiatric hospitalization . . . Joss should begin individual psychotherapy on a three-times-per-week basis. I am available to consult with the Proctors to help find a therapist who is willing to make an intense, long-term commitment to Joss' treatment. Once he is established in psychotherapy, the therapist will coordinate with other professionals to find the best balance of psychotropic medications for him.*

And the remaining recommendations covered the Proctors having counselling to help them respond to the children's concerns and to help them prepare for their visits with me, and finally, that I should seek professional consultation to help me deal with *the "depression resulting from the separation from her children, marital conflicts, and preparations for the rehabilitation of the relationship between herself and the children."*

What marital conflicts? Edward and I didn't have any conflicts, other than those normally experienced in any marriage you care to mention. Just because JP had claimed that we were having problems, that I was a 'battered wife' and so on, everyone suddenly believes that rubbish? And again, without proof, evidence of any kind, testimonials, medical records . . . nothing. Obviously where JP was concerned, his word was law and no-one was going to question it.

My children should be with me. Full stop. I – and Edward – had done nothing at all to cause the boys harm, and never would. Their father, on the other hand, had somehow poisoned them against us, got them to believe all of these hateful accusations they were throwing at us, and damaged them to such an extent that Joss was now in need of extensive and very serious treatment.

And yet, everyone involved appears to take the side of this monster . . .

Chapter seventeen

finding Brand

Michael Keene told us there was absolutely no point trying to go back to court with a report like that. He did say we could get a second opinion and I told him I would only accept someone to do this who was an expert in PAS.

It was up to me now to find someone who really knew their stuff, and so my first move was to contact Richard Gardner's office, who referred me to the Rachel Foundation, a not-for-profit organisation in Maryland run by Pamela Stuart-Mills and Bob Hoch, who set up the Foundation in October 2000 to help abducted and alienated children reintegrate with their families. The Foundation states *"Thousands of children are abducted every year, either physically through kidnapping or emotionally through the 'Abduction of the Mind'."* They use the phrase 'Abduction of the Mind' to mean alienation.

The Rachel Foundation had only been established a couple of weeks earlier, so it was all very new, but they were able to give me the name of Dr Ryan Brand in California, who they thought might be able to help us.

Michael contacted Brand, outlined the facts of the case, and Brand agreed to take it on. I spoke with him and we discussed fees: one thousand dollars a day plus expenses, which would include hotel bills, car hire and so on.

Brand sent his CV through and we agreed to have him on board. He told us he wouldn't be available to us for a couple of months because he was involved with another case. We agreed to wait.

In January 2001, Michael filed a motion with the Sandoval County Court for an independent psychological evaluation. The motion cited inadequacies in Dr Rowe's report, in that he failed to take account of *"several important factors regarding the possible existence of parental alienation"* and the motion then listed these factors as follows:

a) *During their interaction with Respondents* [myself and Edward] *the boys used very vulgar language; the boys had never spoken this way in the presence of Respondents before. The attitude of the boys, particularly Joss, was almost exclusively negative. In abusive situations, there is usually a showing of ambivalence, not simply outright hostility. The boys' use of vulgar language and their overtly negative attitudes are hallmark examples of parental alienation.*

b) *During the interview, Michael Proctor denied having ever engaged in activities like tennis and golf this statement is simply false. The blocking out of positive memories is a clear indicator of parental alienation.*

c) *Dr Rowe indicated that Joss Proctor's 'extensive complaints of sexual abuse were not confirmed' and that the 'accounts of sexual misconduct against the children have not been substantiated'. Dr Rowe does not address this issue any further; the lack of attention given to these allegations ignores the obvious question of how the allegations originated in the first place. A paramount example of parental alienation is when children vividly describe situations that did not occur. This appears to be the case with respect to allegations of sexual abuse.*

d) *During the course of the evaluation, the children used words and phrases of an adult nature (e.g. 'State Penitentiary', 'ignorant', 'you took my childhood away from me') and they called their mother by her first name. This is typical behaviour of alienated children.*

e) *Dr Rowe appears to have discounted evidence and testimonials from outside sources familiar with the boys' life in England. Dr Rowe was provided with numerous letters indicating that the boys were living normal, healthy lives while in England. (Dr Rowe indicated that he did review these materials in preparing his report; nonetheless, there is no reference to any such materials in the body of the report itself.) This evidence, if afforded appropriate weight, would help contradict the allegations of Petitioners* [the Proctors] *and further support the conclusion that the boys have been alienated from Respondents.*

The motion went on to say that the Proctors were present at Rowe's office during our meeting with Rowe, and pointed out that this situation no doubt contributed to what was an already hostile atmosphere:

> *"The presence of an alienating parent is also consistent with parental alienation; the alienating parent creates the illusion that the child will not be safe unless he is present to protect the child from the other parent."*

And a final – immensely professional and concise – statement which summed up what we had been trying to tell all of these people:

> *"The behaviour demonstrated by the children during the evaluation demonstrates clear evidence of parental*

alienation. Before this Court can have a clear understanding of all of the issues, it is necessary for the children to be evaluated by an expert who specializes in parental alienation. The opinion of such an expert will leave no doubt as to whether parental alienation exists in this case."

Michael suggested that, given the extreme opposition we had received from every area, it would carry far more weight if we could fly out and appear in court with Brand. He was dead right. The hearing was set for April 2001.

We met Brand for the first time two days before the hearing, in a hotel room in New Mexico, and we told him our sad story, gave him our 'evidence', such as it was – the photos and letters we seemed to have proffered a hundred times, that so far no-one in this sorry saga had been the slightest bit interested in.

Brand was a man in his mid-fifties, not tall or at all distinguished, but very professional and he immediately took on board what we were trying to explain. He understood what we told him had been going on, as he had dealt with many abductions before this one. Quite early on in our discussions, he said this was all about JP, who he concluded must be suffering from some form of personality disorder.

Dear God, the realisation that we now had someone on our side who realised the truth of the situation, who had experience and knowledge of these things . . . you can't appreciate what that meant to us.

The day of the hearing came and I was terrified. I sat at the back of the Sandoval County Court room, trembling and afraid as if for my life. I knew that, if the court didn't accept Brand, that was it. This would be over once and for all and I would probably never see my boys again.

Michael had been spot on with his guess that there would

be enormous opposition to having Brand on board. He had to plead that the boys had been seen by a total of no less than nine therapists and/or psychologists – all of whom had been sourced and recruited by the Proctors, and we were simply asking for one psychologist of our own choosing.

Eventually, after a hearing that seemed as if it would never end, I sat with my heart in my mouth waiting to hear Judge McDougall's decision. I almost had to pinch myself to make sure I wasn't dreaming when he said they *would* allow Brand to have access to all of the records, and to speak to all of those involved in the case. He would not, however, let him interview the children because that would cause too much psychological damage to them. He did add, amazingly, that this could possibly be arranged for some point further down the road.

Of course, Hoffmann, the boys' lawyer, went to great lengths to try to ensure this didn't happen – he resisted at every turn, arguing that this could cause the boys a massive set-back and it should be taken into account that they were now doing *"so much better"*. It was all I could do not to laugh out loud – after what we had seen recently, they were certainly *not* doing better, they were in the most appalling state, as was clear to anyone who saw them. Also, there was no actual proof that they were improving – because it simply wasn't true.

But the main thing was, we now had the first decision to go in our favour – Brand was being allowed to see all the records and we could meet all of the people who had been involved. We could scarcely believe it.

We arranged to spend a whole week there with Ryan. As we left, brimming with renewed hope, we saw the Proctors in the car park, looking very uncomfortable, speaking to their attorney. For the first time in this hideous charade, something was going our way.

To help Michael prepare the best case possible, I had written to him in detail explaining my responses to all of the points in Rowe's report, which he made use of in the motion filed at court, and I had also enclosed a copy of something written by Douglas Darnall, PhD, as follows:

> *"What does a Severely Alienated Child look like?*
> *They have a relentless hatred towards the targeted parent.*
> *They parrot the Obsessed Alienator.*
> *The child does not want to visit or spend time with the targeted parent.*
> *Many of the child's beliefs are enmeshed with the alienator.*
> *The beliefs are delusional and frequently irrational.*
> *They are not intimidated by the Court.*
> *Frequently, their reasons are not based on personal experience with the targeted parent but reflect what they are told by the Obsessed Alienator.*
> *They have difficulty making any differentiation between the two.*
> *The child has no ambivalence in his feelings; it's all hatred with no ability to see the good.*
> *They have no capacity to feel guilty about how they behave towards the targeted parent or forgive any past indiscretions.*
> *They share the Obsessed Alienator's cause. Together, they are in lockstep to denigrate the hated parent.*
> *The children's obsessional hatred extends to the targeted parent's extended family without any guilt or remorse.*
> *They can appear like normal healthy children until asked about the targeted parent – that triggers their hatred."*
> *(copyright Douglas Darnall, PhD 1998)*

Armed with the court order Ryan had been granted, allowing him access to all files and all professionals involved, we made the best use of the week with him after the hearing, travelling around New Mexico visiting those people we wanted to speak with, and trying to build a picture that would help our case.

Our first stop was the Placitas Elementary School. The Proctors, in the first of many such relocations, had left there in September 2000 and moved to a tiny place called Abiquiu which is in a remote area close to the Colorado border. The headmistress was obviously very loathe to meet us and didn't even bother trying to hide her feelings, no doubt nurtured by the many stories of our evil doings that she would have heard from the Proctors. We had to bear in mind that she had seen the awful state of the boys and that she – along with everyone else concerned – believed, without a shadow of doubt, that we were the terrible perpetrators and totally responsible for all of the awful things Michael and Joss had been through.

After a while, though, she seemed to warm to us slightly and she told us about poor Joss and how he had had a breakdown in the school, how he had suffered paranoid delusions and how this had badly affected the other children – so much so, Joss had had to leave the school.

It was incredibly disturbing for me to have to hear this from a complete stranger, and to know, once again, that I could not have been there when Joss must have needed me in his worst times. He must have suffered so much. I wondered silently just how many times I could feel my heart break before there was nothing left of it to break again.

After this meeting, and with a clear insight of things to come, we drove to the school in Bernalillo, where Joss' teacher told us he had had to have an aide with him full-time because of his anti-social behaviour. She showed us some of the pictures he had drawn – with Edward depicted as the devil. It wasn't easy to meet with these people, knowing they all saw us as the lowest kind of beings imaginable, but we knew we had to go through this if we wanted to get anywhere with the case. Ryan explained to us that the imagery of someone as the devil was a common aspect of the work of severely alienated children. His words, however kindly meant, didn't really help.

Our next port of call was Espanola, further to the north, to the school the children were currently attending. There we met quite a few of the teachers and we learned that both boys were having behavioural problems in school – starting fights, causing problems with other pupils, and so on. We tried to explain that we really were not the root cause of all of this, and that all we wanted was to see the boys healthy and happy once more. But we were playing to a hostile audience, as they, too, must have heard so much rubbish from the Proctors since this all began.

Another meeting was with Lloyd Vogel, the social worker who had been working with the Proctor family. Everything we tried to explain to him went straight over his head. That, we realised, was the common problem here – it was over the heads of most people. No-one had ever known anything so bad, so extreme – and they simply couldn't understand it.

It was during this week's trip around the area meeting with the various professionals, that we became aware of the unbelievably underhand behaviour of some of these people – people you'd expect to be completely 'above board'.

The list of those we had to meet with included Dr Rowe, of course. When he was presented with the court order he said he couldn't meet Ryan that particular week, since he would be out of town on a conference: he offered a meeting on the Sunday, knowing full well that Ryan was to leave on that day. It was only much later, when Rowe sent me a copy of one of his bills covering that period, that it was clear to see that he had had a meeting with the Proctors on the Thursday of the same week. Hardly an out-of-town conference. They had probably panicked on hearing the court ruling and had arranged to see Rowe urgently.

Unsurprisingly, Rowe went to great lengths to avoid the issue – probably hoping we would eventually give up and go away. He must have known that this whole episode was costing us a vast amount of money, not to mention the logistics of constantly travelling back and forth between the UK and the USA, getting Brand to come from another State – and all the while having to organise care for little Dani every time we had to leave home.

Rowe's first attempt to block us was to claim that Brand, being from California, would need to have a New Mexico licence if he was to act as psychologist in this case. Rowe didn't seem to care that the judge had given Brand a court order and full permission to interview all of the professionals. Fortunately, Brand managed to obtain sponsorship from another New Mexico psychologist, Dr Christopher Allander.

This knee-jerk reaction by Rowe to Brand coming on board clearly indicated that Rowe was going to make life as difficult for us as he could. Why was he doing this? Why could he not just be open about his findings and discuss the case with another professional? The obvious conclusion would be that he had something to hide.

Next on our list was the questionable Dr Gomez. We tracked down his office, only to be told by the nurse on duty that Gomez was not there and she sent us off to a completely different address – premises that had been vacated the day before! We returned to the first office where Ryan did find the elusive Doctor and handed him the court order. After that, he never returned any of our calls, nor did he respond to our efforts to actually meet with him.

Moving on, we approached the famous Dr McKay, the person who had set this whole nightmare in motion. She surprised us by agreeing to meet and we arranged an appointment at her office. By the time we arrived, I was shaking with uncontrollable anger, unable to contain my feelings for this woman who had, so irresponsibly, made judgements – based solely on JP's word – that had turned our entire world upside down and had caused me to have my babies taken from me.

I just couldn't help myself as we eventually came face to face and I blurted out the words, *"Why didn't you call me? Do you realise what damage you've caused? How could you have testified in a Federal Court without ever speaking to me – the custodial parent for ten years? . . ."*

I could hear myself, as if from a distance, bombarding her with questions. Poor Ryan had to calm me down. This was such an emotional incident for me, finally meeting this woman who, in my book, had so much explaining to do, and there I was, in her office, barely a few feet from her – I just had to speak my mind.

McKay claimed she had tried to contact me several times but *"couldn't get a connection".* Oh, yes? How pathetic. Where was she, in some third world country where telephones were a luxury enjoyed only by the elite? We all know that telephone communication between the UK and the States is excellent, and she must know that. I asked what had happened to the social services and she replied that they couldn't touch the case because it was outside their jurisdiction. I leapt in again. *"So you took it upon yourself to influence the judges without ensuring the appropriate professional mechanisms were in place?"* I almost shrieked.

I knew this was too little, too late, but I couldn't help it. I was furious and I had every right to be.

Ryan had a meeting with Hoffmann – one professional lawyer to another – to try to get Hoffmann to accept that there could possibly be another explanation for the boys' behaviour, to get Hoffmann to open his mind to the possibility of PAS. This proved to be hopeless. Hoffmann was not going to budge from his opinions. He did acknowledge that, although he had experience of custody cases over twenty years, he had never before witnessed anything like this case. I tried to say that perhaps that meant we were dealing with something very different – a new phenomenon that needed to be addressed differently, and that we should be looking for explanations other than straightforward physical abuse. I added that it didn't make any sense that we kept travelling to the States, facing all kinds of opposition, requesting further hearings, hiring expensive professionals and everything else we could clearly be seen to be doing, if we were guilty. Surely that's just common sense?

No matter, Hoffmann was obviously not moving and we knew that he would be a huge stumbling block for us. But I knew that the whole world could stand against us and I simply could not, would not, give up my fight to get my children back.

By the end of that week of travelling and meetings, punctuated by fierce opposition and brick walls, Ryan had compiled a file of notes, but he still needed to try to influence the judge to allow him to see the boys. This was vital if he was going to be able to produce a valid report.

It was clear that all of the professionals were going to object and try to make it difficult for him. This week had certainly given us a taste of things to come – and it wasn't an attractive scenario.

Ryan returned to California and we flew back to England to catch our breath before going back again a few months later for the hearing when Ryan would ask permission from the court to see the boys. More sleepless nights, more worry, but most of all, more time without my children, not knowing what was happening to them. Not knowing, but most definitely fearing the worst.

Chapter eighteen

against all odds

On the seventh of May, 2001, Michael Keene served Rowe with a subpoena requesting any and all records which had been provided by Edward and myself prior to Rowe's evaluation. This was to include medical records for both of the boys, letters from my father, the boys' school, family, friends and neighbours, photographs, the letter from JP to us and so on. The subpoena requested that all of these documents be supplied to Michael by nine-thirty on the morning of the eleventh of May.

Needless to say, Rowe did not comply and nothing was handed over.

On the tenth of May, Michael attended a deposition of Rowe in another case, and Rowe told Michael that he wouldn't be able to supply these records without an official release from me, and advised that we should extend the deadline until such release was provided. Why couldn't he have mentioned this when Ryan contacted him in April? This was so obviously an attempt at obstruction. We had no choice but to agree to an extended deadline and Michael forwarded the release to Rowe on the eleventh of June, requesting the documents by the new deadline of the second of July.

The second of July arrived and passed by – again, nothing was received. On the same day, Michael forwarded a letter to

Rowe requesting his compliance with the subpoena, giving yet another deadline, this time the thirteenth of July. Yet another date that came and went without any response from Rowe.

On the sixteenth of July, Michael sent a letter to the Guardian Ad Litem, Hoffmann, regarding the behaviour of Dr Rowe, with a copy of that letter going to Rowe himself. Hoffmann then asked Rowe to provide Michael with the documents as required. On the twentieth of July, Michael filed a motion with the Sandoval County Court, detailing all of the above and stating that, as at the date of the motion, Rowe had made no effort to comply with the subpoena.

The motion requested that the Court: *"hold Dr Rowe in contempt, that he be ordered to comply with the subpoena forthwith (but in no event later than five (5) days from the entry of the order), that he be sanctioned and admonished for his disregard of this Court, and that the Court order such other relief as may be just and proper."*

While all of this legal to-ing and fro-ing was going on, a meeting took place in Rowe's office on the fourteenth of June between Hoffmann (the children's guardian), Burke (another of JP's lawyers), Rowe and Michael Keene: this was an informal case discussion. Michael asked if they considered it would be detrimental to the boys if they were to meet with Brand, and suggested that Brand might carry out an evaluation on them. Rowe, of course, immediately on the defensive, declared that it would be damaging; he claimed that Joss would be 'terrified' of another evaluation and that he would find such overwhelming. He added that, if such a meeting were to take place, it would necessitate significant preparation by their current therapists. He also suggested that the boys would see an evaluation by Brand as a 'threat' from their mother and that this would therefore damage even further the relationship between them and me.

Michael went on to ask about PAS and whether Rowe

considered this a possibility in this case. Rowe declared that PAS was definitely not present here, and he said that, in classic PAS cases, the children would not want to see the alienated parent at all, whereas in this instance they were not at all opposed, apparently, to re-establishing a relationship with me, and that the problem for the boys was not with me, but with Edward. Both Rowe and Hoffmann acknowledged that the initial contact had been horrific: Rowe added that, if this was indeed a true PAS case, the boys would not have spoken to me under any circumstances – he said that PAS children take a 'monolithic' attitude towards the alienated parent. Michael, having little or no knowledge of PAS himself, believed that this argument about the children adopting a 'monolithic' attitude towards me, if they had been victims of PAS, would probably carry some weight in court – bear in mind that the judge would also know nothing about PAS. Brand had to challenge this point and explain that the concept was completely wrong – nonsense, in fact.

Hollida Wakefield of the Institute for Psychological Therapies in Minnesota, a psychologist specialising in cases involving allegations of sexual abuse, commented on the child shooting the father in the Lohstroh case: *"The incident illustrated like nothing else the damage that can be done"* to children whose parents accuse each other of wrongdoing during a bitter custody battle. *"When there actually is abuse . . . it's not a typical reaction to hate* [the abuser] *so much you go and shoot him. The typical reaction is one of ambivalence – they love the parent, but they don't like what the parent is doing."* Wakefield added, *"The shooting sounds more characteristic of an extremely alienated child"* rather than one who was abused.

Rowe's advice was that the children's relationship with me should be repaired, and that the boys really did want this to happen. He said visitation should be set up every day – initially supervised but soon progressing to unsupervised. He actually said he believed that the relationship would be repaired quickly, once regular contact could be resumed.

This all proved to be complete rubbish, as we suspected, when I later made two more trips out there; it soon became crystal clear that visitation of any kind wasn't going to work.

When the subject of the allegations of sexual abuse was brought up, Rowe tried to skirt over this, saying that he didn't believe Edward had actually done anything abusive to the boys, but that possibly seeing Edward undressed – perhaps when they went swimming together or even at home getting changed – could have been elaborated to such a degree that the boys then believed as fact that they had been the victims of sexual abuse. He said such elaboration is especially common in children who are in a psychotic state. When it was queried as to why the boys never mentioned any abuse until they were in the States, Rowe brushed this off, saying children in abusive situations can cope with a great deal while they are still in that situation. He had to acknowledge that the boys had exaggerated their experiences when relating them to their father, and he indicated that this was a mechanism used by the boys to ensure they would not be returned to the UK.

Brand responded to all of this by saying it was clearly the adults in the Proctor family who didn't want to have any such involvement by him with the boys, and that they were using trauma to the children as their way of avoiding this, but it was really a fabricated excuse.

The boys had created a situation where they didn't talk to me and they had been refusing to do so: they were being controlled by the Proctors and by Rowe – he demonstrated his lack of any knowledge of PAS and was literally making things up as he spoke, but he was in a position of such authority and influence he simply couldn't be seen to admit any failing, or to back down at this stage. His report, as the appointed psychologist in this case, would influence the court, the judge, the guardian – indeed, everyone involved, and would be of paramount importance in the custody evaluation.

If Rowe had known anything about PAS, he would have realised that the boys' extremely oppositional behaviour towards me, their use of adult terms and phrases such as *"you took my childhood from me"*, *"he belongs in the State Penitentiary"* and so on, calling me by my first name, the accusations of sexual abuse that were totally unfounded – all of this is typical of alienated children. It is *not* how *abused* children behave.

Ryan and Michael had to box clever as Rowe was making this so difficult; the opposition from him and Hoffmann was fierce. They needed to create a second professional opinion to review the case, and to challenge Rowe on the basis of alternative explanations for the conclusions in Rowe's report. Brand presented an idea that might be accepted: he could observe via a two-way mirror during a supervised visitation set up for me with the boys, so he could see how the children reacted towards me and he could make an informed opinion as to the boys displaying signs of alienation. He would not be able to produce a report without seeing the children – this was a vital stage in our progress.

August came around and we flew out again to meet with Ryan Brand. There was an informal meeting with the judge, with both attorneys present, and, to our complete amazement, it was agreed that he could carry out a proper evaluation on the boys – he was being given permission to see them. This was more than we had dared hope for. Although we felt a mild sense of achievement, we had learned by now not to build false hope, and we knew there was still a long way to go.

Ryan and Michael met us outside the courthouse: in the haze of the Mexican summer heat, the car park was full of dust-covered Chevrolet pick-up trucks. As I glanced around,

I noticed JP with his lawyer and his other cronies, all in a huddle – I could see, even from a distance, that they appeared worried. For once, I thought, things haven't gone his way in court. I looked away quickly. I couldn't bear to look at him, I hated him so much.

Ryan met the boys on two occasions during that week. He told us they were definitely displaying all of the hallmarks of alienated children – this was an almost textbook case. Most importantly, the aspect that Rowe had highlighted in error, that the boys were ambivalent towards me, was proved absolutely untrue. Not only did they not show ambivalence, they really hated me and that was all there was to it. They actually told Ryan that the only thing I was good for was being *"a vessel that gave birth to them"*.

We spent a lot of time with Ryan that week, and he related to us some of the cases he had handled in the past where the circumstances were relevant to what we were witnessing with the boys. We learned a lot from him about the murky world of child abduction, about people being drawn into various cults, how it took professional involvement to help de-program them, once they were rescued from the grip of mind control . . . he had many such stories and he explained that victims of PAS are treated very much the same as adults who are caught up in cults where they are totally controlled. He also knew that PAS was most effective with children aged between nine and twelve: Joss was eleven and Michael was ten at the time.

All of this was incredibly interesting, even in my state of distress, and I listened intently: I wanted to learn as much as I could, and I remember thinking what a far cry this was from my life as a housewife in southern England, driving across New Mexico learning about brainwashing, but it was all so relevant.

Ryan met with Rowe, finally, when the elusive Doctor could no longer run and hide, and he asked to see all of the psychological tests Rowe had carried out on the adults. Rowe handed them over – all except the tests on JP, surprise, surprise. Rowe said he had lost those. How on earth could a professional, dealing with something so sensitive, lose one set of tests from a batch that should have been kept together at all times? This had to be a cover-up; there was some reason why Rowe didn't want another psychologist to see those tests. All of the others – my own, Edward's and Tess Proctor's – showed nothing out of the ordinary and were completely normal.

I am quite certain that something came up in the missing tests that would have contradicted Rowe's theory, and – instead of admitting this and being professional – Rowe took the easy route away from any potential doubts as to his credibility in the case.

To this day, there has never been any explanation about the missing tests. No-one else has ever seen them. None of the other professionals seemed at all bothered about this, which I found astonishing. It was all just swept under the carpet, like so many issues, and it wasn't even brought up in the court case which was to follow.

Another meeting for Ryan this week was with the Proctors. They met in a hotel room at two in the afternoon, and Tess was very clearly drunk. She was slurring her words, swaying in her seat and when Ryan offered her some documents, she snatched the papers out of his hands. It was also apparent to Ryan that JP was telling a lot of lies.

A date was then set for the court hearing in January 2002. It seemed an awfully long time away and my disappointment lay heavily on me. Another half a year without my children, not even a telephone call. It had already been twenty months – almost two years – since the children had been taken from me, and now I was facing another five months of emotional torture. I felt physically sick and all my energy drained from me in a huge subsiding wave. How much more of this could

I take? Not to see or hear from your children when they are so young is a pain like no other, for any mother.

Michael explained that this time was absolutely necessary for everyone to prepare the case for court. Ryan also had his report to compile and produce, now that he had finally seen the children. We discussed the financial arrangements, agreeing to pay Michael and his legal partner, David Crane, a fee of twenty thousand dollars; Ryan required a minimum of fifteen thousand dollars.

Everything in place, we set off back to England, home once more. The difference this time was that we had some hope now – with Michael and Ryan very much on side and Ryan's forthcoming report to take to court, we felt we had had a successful trip, for once. All we could do now was wait out the months until the new year.

New year, new hope.

Chapter nineteen

preparing for court – no straight answers

In preparing his report, Ryan collated all of the statements and other information he had gathered from the service providers in the States, all of the material we had given him, and he then diligently contacted and interviewed as many of the appropriate parties in the UK as he possibly could – several of the teachers at the boys' school, the headmaster, our neighbours, parents of friends of the boys, my father and others. It was, indeed, a relief for us to see that what should have been done a long time ago was actually being done now: surely, all of this would definitely have some effect on the court's attitude to the case? Strange, don't you think, that Ryan managed to get through to the UK every time he tried, when Dr McKay had said it was impossible.

With all of this information to hand, Ryan prepared and wrote his report.

Meanwhile, Michael's next task, as part of his own preparation, was to depose the Proctors. This means holding a court hearing and asking them questions under oath and having the session recorded by a recognised professional court reporter. Shortly after the trial, we were supplied with copies of these depositions – they make very interesting reading.

Let me illustrate firstly with some extracts – and these are verbatim, I assure you – from the deposition of Mrs Tess Proctor. Please note that the letter 'Q' signifies a question being posed by our lawyer, Michael Keene, and 'A' signifies her response.

Michael had just submitted a student behaviour survey on Joss dated the twenty-seventh of March, 2001, which had been taken by the school he was attending, and he pointed out a statement made by Joss, "*. . . and my mom washes my mouth out with soap and talks to me*". Michael asked "*Is there any truth in this?*"

A. *Yes.*
Q. *How often have you done that?*
A. *Once.*
Q. *Once? And why was that?*
A. *What part are you talking about?*
Q. *Sorry, let me clarify that.*
A. *Please.*
Q. *"wash my mouth out with soap"*
A. *Once.*
Q. *Once? And why was that?*
A. *The language he used was just – I had tried all other techniques of controlling his speech, you know, his bad language, and it wasn't working, and I said "maybe if we clean that mouth out" and I . . . you know, I did it.*

Michael knew that the boys were often left in the 'care' of JP's domineering mother, and he asked about which members of the family were at home at different times . . .

Q. *How often does John travel?*
A. *When? I mean . . .*
Q. *On average, per month.*
A. *Per month?*

Q. *How often is he away from the home?*
A. *If he's gone . . . That's a big 'if', maybe one night.*

On a different subject, but still Tess didn't seem capable of giving a direct answer to a question . . .

Q. *Give me an example of a time when he [Joss] lied to you. What did he lie about?*
A. *I don't know. I mean, there is so many . . . I'm just sort of getting confused here.*

Throughout the whole deposition session, there was so much attempting to evade questions, not to give direct answers. But why? If they had been in the right, why not tell all as it was? Even the simplest question seemed to cause more confusion.

Q. *Do you drink or experiment with illegal drugs?*
A. *Which question are you asking?*

But all of that was nothing when compared to JP's deposition. On the subject of custody and visitation rights, Michael had asked JP what his specific visitation rights were, as laid down by the court.

A. *I believe . . . and I haven't read the documents in a long time, but I believe*
when I was in England I could come and visit them as often as I wanted
to.
Q. *Was the visitation order ever modified preceding January 2000 when this case began?*
A. *I don't know. I can't recall.*

He was saying he actually didn't remember something so vitally important as his legal rights to see his own children, who were living on the other side of the planet?

Q. *What was the child support order?*
A. *This is a guess, but I believe the child support order called for me paying five thousand dollars a month . . . and I think there was some other thingsbut I can't remember what else.*

Can't remember? How important is it to know what sums of money you are supposed to be paying – as ordered by the court? Obviously not at all to him.
Michael knew this was an area that would, hopefully, show JP in his true colours, as he hadn't paid the child maintenance since May 1991. Hardly the sign of a loving, caring father?

Q. *And there was a confirmed arrearage of fifty-six thousand dollars? Does that sound right, subject to an assignment?*
A. *I believe so.*
Q. *What was the assignment?*
A. *I can't remember.*

Then Michael asked JP when he had last made a payment of child maintenance, and, suddenly, JP's lawyer interjected. *"I'm going to object on the basis of relevance, but go ahead and answer"*.

A. *It would be purely a guess, though, I would say.*
Q. *Okay. Can you make a guess as to how much you were still in arrears?*
A. *No, I cannot.*

As if he wouldn't remember the considerable amount of money he owed in child support, or when he had last paid anything.

When asked what he did for a living, JP described an Irish company, New Millenia Biosciences, and explained briefly that this was an agrochemical business in developmental stages of products.

Q. *Do you have a job title?*
A. *I believe they call me CEO.*

What? The man doesn't know his own job title? He isn't aware that he apparently holds one of the highest positions that exist in a US business? Staggering.

Michael asked how much JP was earning from this work, and there followed the most complicated and determined attempt to avoid any real answer . . .

Q. *How much do you earn per month?*

Here, JP's lawyer butted in again, saying they were going to leave the court for a while, which they did, then JP continued.

A. *I am provided on a monthly basis, in the form of loans, moneys to allow me to pay for my living expenses.*
Q. *Is that something which you eventually will have to pay back?*
A. *Yes.*
Q. *How much do you get in loans per month?*
A. *We have a list of expenditures that we get on the average.*

And then there was a listing of the Proctors' household bills, medical costs, vehicle costs, children's clothes . . . why could the man not simply have had a figure ready, instead of dragging everyone through a maze of what cost how much, how often, ad hoc expenses and the like? Because you can't hide behind straight facts, you can only hide behind messy scenarios that throw everyone off the scent. He threw in a figure which he said was a contribution from his parents each month, he explained that his mortgage was not in his name, but the company's. Even when a total of sorts was reached to represent the monthly outgoings, JP still had to argue . . .

> Q. *Is it fair to assume that you earn more than five thousand dollars per month, if that's what you're paying out?*

JP's lawyer stepped in again with *"Objection, argumentative."* And JP said *"I don't understand the question. I am . . . I don't earn it."*

> Q. *Let me tell you where I'm going with this. This may make it easier.*
> A. *I borrow it. That's not earnings to me.*

He would not give in. Even the simplest question was answered with doubt, query, twisted facts. 'I think . . . I believe . . . I guess . . . I don't know.' How could he be so utterly vague about so many things, so many vitally important things?

When Michael attempted to glean information about what JP's earnings would be, once the company had completed development and had become productive, once again JP's lawyer, Burke, spoke out with yet another objection.

Given that the entire court proceedings were based around JP's fabricated notification of child abuse, you would expect he had prepared himself at least with the basic facts of his initial approach to the court. Referring to the pleadings filed by JP on the sixth of January, 2000, which had kick-started this whole evil charade, Michael tried to get JP to explain what had transpired. He referred to the content of the *Petition for Emergency Protective Order*, quoting *"the abuse has been reported to the New Mexico Child Welfare Department"* and asking JP whether it was he or Dr McKay who had reported the 'abuse'. And still, like some slithering snake in the grass, moving this way and that, JP replied *"I believe possibly both of us."*

Michael asked him if he had ever received a letter from the child protection authorities telling him that the case had been dismissed, or if it had been substantiated, or anything similar. His reply – *"I can't recall."*

When the questions moved on to the actual allegations of abuse, JP suddenly became animated, his speech more detailed, his replies much lengthier. He had obviously learned by heart all of the lies and exaggerations, the accusations and the descriptions – he must have thought this part of the proceedings was where he needed to take centre stage, to 'capture his audience'. The bits that had gone before were obviously boring to him, of no interest, but this was the meaty part that would allow him to use his skill as a creative liar, coming across as totally credible, winning everyone over to his side.

He described the awful state of the boys 'every time' he saw them – wearing dirty clothes, ill-fitting clothes that were unwashed, not ironed, dirty hair, they hadn't brushed their teeth for 'probably weeks on end'. He said the first thing they ever did when the boys arrived was to get them cleaned, washed, bathed and taken to the barber shop. He even said their finger and toenails were uncut and in-growing.

All utter rubbish, of course.

He tried to win sympathy by saying there was a period of two years when *"I could not afford to bring them over"* so he didn't get the chance to see them for that time. He forgot to add that, as well as not receiving any child support from him, each time the boys did fly out to stay with him, I was the one footing the bill for air fares.

He said he had confronted me over the condition of the boys and that my response was that I *"couldn't be bothered"*. His excuse for not having pressed the point with me was that he was worried that, if pressured about it, I would *"take it out on the boys"* and not allow them to go to him again.

He said I was having *"difficulties with her family"* – if by difficulty he meant I had an incredibly supportive father who provided me and the boys with a home when I returned to England and the maintenance payments due from him did not materialise, and that my father then proceeded to pay for all of the court cases, professionals' fees, expenses and so on that this nightmare had cost so far – then yes, he was dead right.

He accused Edward of having lived illegally in the States for ten years and then being *"kicked out"* back to England. Rubbish.

The list of lies just goes on and on throughout the entire deposition, and you can tell from his increasingly lengthy and detailed responses to questions that he was loving every minute of it.

We left the children in the car on hot days, according to JP, who backed up the accusation with *"I had heard about the fact that kids and dogs could die in cars if you have the windows rolled up and it's hot, you know."* We were drunks, rolling around and vomiting all over the house, and this was one accusation he obviously enjoyed, as he went on *". . . Edward and Pamela would fall down dead drunk and puke all over the living room or puke in the bedroom or puke on the stairs going up or puke behind the couch or that Edward would go out in the front yard and puke and throw up."* I'm sorry, but, even for an experienced drunk, that's a heck of a lot of puking.

He told them that Joss had had to have nine teeth removed and named the dentist who apparently did this work – no doubt someone else he had cajoled or bullied into lying for him.

I was a *"battered wife"*, Edward *"periodically beat"* me and – apparently because I was afraid of what Edward would do to me when he was sober – I hit him *"while he was drunk"*.

I was *"in denial of the fact that she was being battered"* and I blocked it out because I didn't want to *"admit to the world that she's living with a bum".*

– a litany of lies

And so it went. Page upon page of absolute lies. And no scrap of proof, of course, but JP must have thought he was so good at this that he didn't need it.

Then, the topic of the alleged sexual abuse. Obviously JP's personal favourite, as you can tell from the now very lengthy and incredibly detailed answers to all questions. As if he were obsessed with the subject.

He said Joss would hug female friends in *"an inappropriate way, not a way that a child of ten years old . . . you know, how you would hug your son"*. When asked if he could give an example of something inappropriate, he went into minute detail: *"Yeah. When he would hug a woman, he would try to go for the nipple. He would try to go for the breast. He would try to fondle the breast. If he would hug a man, he would touch you in the lower areas and in a way that you would touch somebody if you were having sex with them or something else like that . . ."*

One of his most outrageous lies was that Joss had suffered a dislocated hip – news to me, of course, and there was never one shred of evidence to support this in any of the court hearings. But his point was *"My son was treated for a dislocated hip, which is pretty common in sexual abuse cases."*

He obviously considered me – as he did most people – stupid and totally lacking even in common sense. But I do insist that I would have spotted a dislocated hip in my son, and so would other people around us. He would have been in agony, unable to walk or move around without great pain. JP said Joss had undergone treatment for this condition – where, which doctor, where were the medical records? As always – nothing to support any of it. And – more amazingly – no-one throughout the whole round of court cases, depositions, court orders and so on, ever asked for any evidence.

After JP had spouted all of his fantasies with reference to the sexual abuse, the topic changed again and – strangely – he lapsed back into giving shorter answers and being unable to provide the information being requested. For example, he didn't know how many students there were in Joss' class at school – even though Joss was in a special needs class. He couldn't tell how many sessions Michael had had with McKay or how many with another therapist – whose surname he didn't know. Whenever he couldn't answer, he would say they needed to speak to Tess about whatever it was.

He couldn't recall the name of the special teacher Joss had when receiving home schooling – even though this lady was at his house every day! When asked what extra-curricular activities or sports Michael was involved in, his answer was *"Science"*. He didn't know the name of Joss' current therapist, and referred to her simply as 'Deena'. On the question of Michael having friends to socialise with, he side-stepped this by explaining that they lived in an area where people's homes were not close together and so it wasn't an option for the boys to 'hang out' with other children, unless they were at a special event such as a basketball game.

Michael mentioned that Joss had told McKay at one point that he had a photographic memory and asked JP if this were true. He didn't have a clue.

A. Joss said something like that? I don't know. Ask him, find out. I would not . . .
Q. I don't think anybody is going to let me talk to Joss. To your knowledge, does he have a photographic memory?
A. No. I don't know that. I can't say.

Whenever an opportunity presented itself for JP to revert to mentioning the 'abuse' – for instance, when discussing the boys' medications or behavioural issues – off he'd go once more, talking at great length and providing incredible detail.

There is another very strange part of this deposition that begs to be questioned, and you don't have to be a psychiatrist to spot this one.

Michael asked JP, on the subject of disciplinary measures undertaken by JP or his wife with the boys, *"Have you ever had an occasion to discipline either Joss or Michael?"*

> A. *Oh, yeah . . .*
> Q. *Can you give me some examples of when? Let's start with Joss, two or three examples.*
> A. *Probably one of the most upsetting experiences that we ever had with Joss was Joss would relay the intimate aspects of his sexual life in England at inappropriate times, or he would go into fits that we were told was caused by his post traumatic stress disorder. The longest fit was 14 hours, and I had to prevent him from hurting himself, to physically restrain, to hold him. So that these occasions . . . I mean, you can't get mad at somebody who's going through those kind of flashbacks. You just have to love them.*

Apart from the fact that he deviated totally from what was being asked, was he actually admitting that he had 'disciplined' Joss for what was basically mental health problems? More worrying is that he refers to what he insists all along is sexual abuse against his children as their 'sexual life', as if they were adults. His use of the word 'somebody' again suggests an adult, rather than a little boy.

This complete diversion from any appropriate response to a question about discipline was – what? His desire to avoid discussing the subject? Why? Or, more likely, JP using yet more stories of the boys' problems to gain sympathy? Who knows what was going on in his mind?

Michael repeated the question, determined to get JP to answer, but all he got was a vague admission that there was some form of discipline but this was along the lines of 'time out' or 'take a nap', and he again deferred to his wife as the one who was *"really more responsible for the day-to-day disciplinary action . . ."*

All of this vagueness and repeatedly passing the buck to Tess – was this his way of preparing in case things did go against him in the end? Would it then appear that she was the one who had caused the problems?

On page sixty-one of his deposition, JP proudly announces, referring to Joss, that *"we know everything about him because we make it our issue to do so"*. Two pages further on, he was asked when Joss had started at Espanola Middle School and he replied *"Last year"*. Michael asked if that meant the beginning of the 2001 school term, in September or August, and JP replied *"Yeah, right"*.

At this incredible mistake, JP's own lawyer interjected, correcting his statement and advising that he should have said September of the year 2000.

So much for 'knowing everything about Joss'.

Also on page seventy, he was asked what type of therapy Joss was currently receiving.

A. *Joss has therapy from . . . It used to be Lloyd Vogel. It's now someone by the name of Deena, and she sees him on a regular basis. Occasionally we take him to McKay, but most of the time it's with the therapist that's provided to us by the State.*

That sounds rather casual and disorganised for something as crucial as therapy for a child.

Q. *Is Joss on any medication?*
A. *Absolutely.*
Q. *What does he take?*
A. *Again this is Paxil and Risperdal, I believe, and one other.*

I believe? One other? Surely you'd have details of what heavy medication your child was being prescribed for mental health problems?

Michael produced a document which he handed to JP, saying it was a *Sentence Completion Series* which was completed by Joss in the year 2000. He asked JP to confirm that this was the information he could see on the front page.

A. *Yes, I do. So that's his first . . . you know more than I do as to when he started going to Espanola.*
Q. *Fair enough. This looks like a woman's handwriting. This is not Joss' handwriting answering the questions, is it, to your knowledge?*
A. *It looks like Joss', yeah. Now that doesn't look like it.*

So – this man who 'knows everything' about his son, Joss, doesn't know the name of his current therapist, nor does he know what medication the boy is on. And, to add to this amazing range of knowledge about his child, when Michael asked if anyone else, apart from Dr Gomez, was prescribing medication for Joss, he replied *"No, not to my knowledge"*.

So, to sum up, this man who says he has made it his business to know everything about his son, has failed on the following points:

He doesn't know what his visitation rights are as per the court order

He doesn't know what was laid down in the child support order

He doesn't know how much unpaid child support he owes

He doesn't know if the CPS ever carried out an investigation following his contact with them to complain about child abuse

He doesn't know what medication his son is taking

He doesn't know who might be prescribing medication for his son

He doesn't know with which therapist his son is having therapy

He doesn't know if his son has a photographic memory or not

He doesn't know how often his son has to be disciplined

He doesn't know when his son started his current school

He doesn't know how many pupils were in the special needs class

and

He doesn't recognise his own son's handwriting

How is it, that I can see right through this man, this vile creature so full of lies, accusations, schemes . . . this person who has caused so much heartache to so many people, including his own flesh and blood – when no-one else, before we found Michael and Ryan, thought to question anything he said?

But at least we *had* found them – and at this point, they were my hope.

Chapter twenty

2002 court case – two days of my life

January 2002 arrived. We flew out again and met up with Ryan and Michael, who explained how the case would proceed. Michael said day one would be for the Proctors and Dr Rowe to testify, then the second day would give us our turn with Ryan. We had a fair idea of what JP and Tess would be saying from the depositions, of which we had been given copies.

That night, Edward and I stayed at a little hotel called La Posada in downtown Albuquerque – an old-fashioned place full of character and very stylish. We felt that we needed to be in comfortable surroundings to at least attempt to get a decent night, and it was a lovely place. There was a chap playing piano in the evening, which was really pleasant – not that we were in any mood for such entertainment and relaxation, given what was ahead of us.

One more restless night of terrifying thoughts, fear and dread . . . and that pit-of-the-stomach sickness, then the day dawns and stark reality hits me like a runaway truck. I try to pull the ragged edges of my mind together to prepare for the onslaught of another court hearing.

But this time it was *the* court hearing, the one that would, once and for all time, decide the fate of my children. And mine, too.

We drove in our hire car to the little courthouse in Bernalillo, just beyond the outskirts of Albuquerque. The assortment of workmen's trucks in the car park illustrated very clearly the usual business of this court – petty crime, small-time legal issues and local family custody cases. This was not a court with any experience of hugely complex international custody hearings. I was terrified – physically shaking. My feet were walking along the ground but I was not aware of being in control of the movement: it was as if I were in a trance.

This was to be the most vitally important two days of my entire life. The judge would not realise this, but the outcome of this hearing would determine whether or not I would ever see my boys again. By now, I had sufficient knowledge of PAS to know that, without appropriate intervention, the boys could not break free of the 'brainwashing'. Two years of waiting and preparing, and the time was finally here. I was relieved to feel so numb, so removed from the physical aspect – I would not get through this any other way.

As we entered the building with Michael Keene and David Crane, I could see people I recognised. JP's parents, Bill Krantz, JP himself and wife Tess. I avoided looking in their direction – I couldn't bear to make eye contact with any of them. Thank God, I now had these decent, professional, intelligent people on my side. I felt enormous gratitude for their support. Ryan joined us shortly afterwards.

In the courtroom, people were taking their seats, chatting, looking at notes. And then silence. The Honourable Lewis P. McDougall, District Court Judge, is presiding.

Burke opened the proceedings and his first words were an attempt to play down the true stature of the case. He said that, although the case had *"an international flavour"*, it was basically the same as those cases normally heard in this court.

It most definitely was not.

I sit, completely still, hardly daring to breathe. After what seems a long time, I am aware of people moving around. JP is taking the stand: he sits, swears the Oath, and then JP's lawyer, Burke, begins his cross-examination.

To start with, things go pretty much as per the deposition, with JP explaining how he doesn't actually earn any money, how he is paid in loans, and the fact that the house he and the family live in is owned by the business. All very convenient for someone who owes thousands of dollars in unpaid child support. He describes this perfect all-American family life of theirs – everyone baking cakes together, big family Sunday dinner, always saying prayers together. Then he tells of a telephone conversation between me and the boys after which Joss apparently had a fit that lasted fourteen hours. He says that's when Dr McKay recommended that contact with me should cease.

Your child has a fit that goes on for fourteen hours? And you don't seek any medical or other expert help or advice? You just allow the child to remain in whatever state for all that time? Would a normal parent not begin to be very concerned after a certain length of time?

When asked how he discovered that the boys were being mistreated in the UK, JP replies that, at Christmas 1998 when the boys were with him for the holiday, *"the kids basically told myself, my wife, Michael Bolton and other people that they were being whipped on a pretty regular basis . . . that Edward would come home drunk and that's when they would get the worst of it."* He says he asked Michael Bolton what he could do, given that the children were UK citizens and that custody of them was in the UK, and he had been told the only way to resolve the situation properly would be to travel to the UK and fight in the English courts.

143

Replying to the question of whether he had brought up the subject with me and Edward, he says he had, but the boys reported to him in 1998 that *"Edward didn't give a damn about me asking him to consider his discipline with the kids."* He added that he became so concerned that he gave the boys a telephone number in case they needed to contact him *"in an emergency"* while they were in the UK, but the boys didn't ever call him because, they told him, I had discovered the number and taken it from them.

JP is putting on such a display of the concerned and loving father, and he pleads *"I thought, what happens if Edward gets so mad at them that he hits them? What if we can't get them over here?"* even adding at one point that he feared Edward might even kill the boys. *"They were in a state of panic, they were so frightened."* His lies have no limits.

In an attempt to draw attention away from his earlier statements about knowing of the abuse in previous years, he explains that the arrival of the boys for their Christmas 1999 holiday was *"completely different from the Christmas before . . . daddy, help us! We don't want to go back! It was tearful, emotional, pleading."*

How about this for evading the reality of the situation? JP is telling the court that yes, he had promised us a payment of child support, but, because the boys were in such an appalling mental state, *". . . when I found out what the situation was, Your Honour, I spent the money on paying for therapists and legal expenses and other things, and I did not send them the money."*

He says that, when the boys first arrived, Joss would regularly talk about death and violence, giving the example, *"If he saw a balloon in the sky at the balloon festival, he'd say 'wouldn't it be great to take a rocket launcher and blast that son-of-a-bitch right out of the sky?'"* but he says now Joss has mellowed and doesn't have the prolonged fits he used to have.

144

On being asked how the boys feel about me and Edward now, he replies, *"The kids genuinely want . . . if Edward was not in the equation at all . . . to somehow re-establish the relationship . . . they do not feel toward Pam as they do toward Edward . . . They have been concerned about Pam's welfare all along . . . She may be hit or in some way violated by his violent behaviour in this sense, OK? And they don't understand why she can't see the light as it relates to Edward. They just hate it. I mean totality."*

> The lies keep on pouring out of JP's mouth and I have to sit, with poor Edward – who is the object of most of the venom – and not speak, not react. It's as if he has robbed me of my children and now he wants to wreck my marriage as well. Luckily, we are stronger than that.

Next, Michael Keene cross-examines JP. Suddenly, it becomes blatantly obvious that there are glaring discrepancies in his statement regarding the timeline of when certain events took place. He claims that, as far back as 1996, he had confronted me about the 'abuse'. He says he had had suspicions and that he contacted the Child Protection Service in 1996 after an alleged incident when I was supposed to have locked the boys in my car for a long period of time. He adds that, even though he sought the help of the CPS, he didn't want custody at that point.

> According to JP, he was so convinced that abuse was taking place that he called the CPS – and yet he was not even interested in taking his children into his own home, to get them away from the 'abusers'. Why would anyone not want custody? Wouldn't that be your first thought? I am asking myself if anyone else is finding this as ridiculous as I am. I can only hope – I start to think about the professionals

on my side, and how diligent they have been so far. Surely they will be able to tear JP's testimony to shreds?

This is where JP gets himself into a real muddle, because in his deposition he had claimed that he did want to switch custody prior to 1999: he even claimed that, back in 1996, he had checked out the Hague Convention rulings but he had been told that if he took that route he could not possibly win – and it would have cost a lot of money to do so. If you – or any parent – had real suspicions that your children were being abused, would money stand in your way? And would you then leave those children in the same place where you had reason to believe the abuse was taking place? With the same people you thought were abusing them? Would you leave them there *for a further three years?* For the whole of that three years, JP made no attempt to contact the boys' school, their GP – in fact, he made no effort to do anything – and, yet, here he sits declaring to the world that he had grave concerns about the children being abused for all of that time. This doesn't make any sense.

Michael's response to this is to stress that there would have had to be allegations of *extreme* abuse for the case to have been heard in New Mexico, which is what had happened.

Something else that makes no sense – why did JP write that letter to me and Edward in August 1997, telling us how grateful he was for the wonderful job we were doing with the boys, how he wanted to repay us, to make it up to us, and so on?

Now he's talking about the time at the Mexican restaurant when he and his pal, Bill Krantz, had collected the boys from the airport and the boys were – according to him – in such an awful state, not properly dressed, scruffy, dirty, and almost hysterical, when they *"started to blurt out"* about the abuse they were suffering at home, where the beatings had *"actually gotten worse, not better, and the beatings were now buckles on the end of belts"*. He says this scene was so bad that other people in the restaurant got up and left without finishing their meals.

> Why would you take one of your employees with you to pick up your children from the airport? Why would you take children who were in such a terrible state into a restaurant? You would not. Simple as that. But there he sat, pouring out lie after incredible lie to the court.

I'm actually starting to consider that Michael is doing a really good job of showing JP to be the despicable liar he is. Nothing he says makes any sense – surely the court will see that? Michael is talking about the amended petition in May 2000 now, and he gets JP to read aloud the part that says there were additional claims being made for *"actual, hedonic and consequential damages"*. JP then asks what this means. Michael says *"That's not my job – you wrote it."* It's all I can do, not to laugh aloud.

> In this same petition it was stated that the emotional problems the boys were experiencing would, in Dr McKay's opinion, necessitate eight years of on-going therapeutic treatment. Based on costs at the time, this therapy would cost fifteen hundred dollars a month. When you add it up, what an amazing coincidence! How strange! It comes to the same amount, almost exactly, as the amount of unpaid child support JP owed to me at the time. How could anyone not see through this charade?

Now it's the turn of Tess Proctor. I look at her and am instantly struck by her demeanour. She must be either drunk or under the influence of drugs: she is slow and laconic, not to mention she is speaking absolute rubbish. As with JP's outpourings, there are serious discrepancies between what she is saying now and what was taken down in her deposition. She says it took six days for the boys to travel from Houston to Albuquerque, whereas in her deposition she said the journey took two days. Just a slight difference. She tells the court my son, Michael, plays varsity basketball. How can he possibly play what is university level sport when he's only twelve years old? She keeps asking *"Is that a question?"* She can't remember it was 1999 when the boys started to live with them, nor can she recall what she said to Dr Rowe.

Am I now hearing things, or did she just say the boys didn't know how to use a knife and fork when they first arrived, and they couldn't dress themselves? My God, this is almost laughable.

Bill Krantz is taking the stand now. He just repeats pretty much what he had related in the original trial, saying what an awful state the boys were in when he and JP picked them up from the airport, how they were dirty and unkempt, how they were really upset and how they were telling of their 'abuse' in the restaurant. Michael asks Krantz if he thinks it is at all strange that JP allowed the boys to carry on, talking loudly about their terrible experiences in front of everyone in the restaurant. He queries why JP didn't take the boys out of the place or take them to one side. Of course, Krantz has nothing to say to this.

First professional witness to take the stand is Charlotte McKay. The questioning begins and she tells the court she met with the Proctors on the twenty-ninth of December, 1999, in order to spend some time with the boys so that she could determine whether or not their statements were credible, and to advise if another evaluation was necessary. During her session with them, Joss and Michael told her they had been left in a car on their own, they were slammed against walls, the police had been called out to the house, and all of those other lies they had so obviously been taught to repeat. McKay says she considered these statements could be true . . .

> Considered? What the hell does that mean? Why did she not try to find some hard evidence to prove or disprove these evil accusations? She had nothing to go on and yet she had somehow managed to produce that report – the report that had condemned us.

. . . but she couldn't form any conclusions from her meetings with the children, so she had approached several Child Protection Services officers – including one in Washington DC – who all told her the case was outside their jurisdiction. She was given some telephone numbers in the UK but she says she couldn't get a connection at the time. She had testified in a Federal Court even though she was not an evaluator and could not make professional recommendations.

> That's it? No connection? And so it's OK, nothing serious enough to keep trying until you do get through? Just the lives of two small children at stake. I've only been in this damned place half an hour and I'm almost at screaming point. I must try to keep it together . . .

McKay continues. She explains that, by March 2000, Joss was having serious problems and on the eleventh of March she administered the Rorschach test for him. This is a psychological test in which the subject is shown various ink-blot images and their interpretation of the images is analysed. The results are used to examine personality and emotional functioning. This can detect underlying thought disorder. Joss saw Edward as the devil when shown the images and he scored positive for schizophrenia. He was having paranoid thoughts and had to

149

be taken out of school; although hospitalisation was recommended at this time, the Proctors took him to see Dr Gomez, who prescribed medication.

> At this point, Dr Rowe enters the courtroom and sits down. The attorneys then get together in a huddle with the judge and they speak in hushed voices – we can't hear what they are saying.[4]

McKay says she doesn't have very much experience of court cases. She claims she wasn't told until the very end of the interview with the Proctors that I was the sole custodian of the children, and that's when she was given my contact numbers. She says she felt that contact with me should be the role of an evaluator, plus she wanted to restrict her involvement. She says she had no idea what course this was going to take.

> Having to sit silently, listening to this woman again is making my blood boil, but I know I can't react or speak. Frustration. How can she say she wanted to limit her involvement when she had been sufficiently involved to testify in Federal Court? She must have known her testimony could sway the court's decision: she knew the boys could be kept in New Mexico for an extended period of time. I grit my teeth as she speaks again.

Her information, she claims, was based on what she gleaned from her meetings with the Proctors and the boys, and she had listened to some extremely negative statements. She says

---

4   I was to discover years later, when I eventually managed to get hold of the taped transcripts from the court, that this conversation was basically the attorneys asking for Rowe to be removed from the court because there were discrepancies between his testimony and McKay's. The judge and Hoffmann said Rowe should remain in court.

she was aware that JP had had the boys with him for only a very short time, and that he wanted to keep them with him in New Mexico.

Surely to God, hearing that should have spurred her into finding out more? Even if she had felt it inappropriate to contact me, what about the boys' teachers in the UK, their doctor – anyone? But she would have needed my permission to do so.

Now McKay is explaining about the Achenbach Behavioural Checklist, the system used to evaluate maladaptive behaviours and emotional problems. It provides an assessment of internalising and externalising behaviours: internalised behaviours cover anxiety, depression, excessive control; externalised behaviours cover aggression, hyperactivity, non-compliance and lack of control. This Checklist also measures social withdrawal, somatic complaints, anxiety and depression, destructive behaviour, social problems, thought problems, attention problems, aggressive and delinquent behaviours. It is compiled of one hundred and thirteen questions on negative behaviour: Joss had scored sixty-five out of one hundred and thirteen, which included such things as being cruel to animals and some severe physical problems; Michael scored fifty out of one hundred and thirteen, including aspects like aches, vomiting and bed-wetting.

McKay had relied on this Checklist and had included it in her letter for the Federal Court. She really should have followed up on this to find out if the boys' behaviours were the same in the UK. Joss, apparently, had a bloody nose due to the 'daily abuse' and yet she never examined any of his medical records. This Achenbach Checklist is meant to be an observation carried out over a six-month period – and yet JP had taken only two weeks to make the assessment which was then accepted. There were issues relating to school that he had completed in the Checklist, and yet he couldn't possibly have known the real details.

McKay tells the court she had to contact the CPS for two reasons: one, because she is required to do so by law; two, the CPS have trained and qualified professionals who are experienced in carrying out such investigations. This is a very dangerous area to delve into because false accusations still have to be followed up and – as we have all read in various cases covered by the press – can result in dreadful outcomes for those concerned. In matters of child protection, any and all accusations or suspicions have to be investigated until it is absolutely clear and certain what the true situation is. But, if the accusations are cleverly constructed and the children are under the influence of the accuser, it can be impossible for any true picture to be drawn.

A letter is produced that McKay had written to Ryan in which she stated that Rowe had never discussed with her the contact she had had with the boys; nor did he ever see any of her notes relating to her involvement with them. She admits that Rowe should have addressed these issues.

Hoffmann, the GAL, cross-examines her and nothing new comes to light, except she claims that, if the case had been more extreme, she would have brought more professionals into the arena to work with her as a team.

More extreme? What is this woman's definition of extreme? Could anything be more extreme than this? And Hoffmann's obvious lack of enthusiasm in the way he is conducting the cross-examination tells me he really is not interested in this case.

Richard Gardner, MD, acclaimed PAS authority, when explaining how the therapist's role in a PAS case should work, says *"The therapist needs input from both parents. The therapist needs input from the victimized parent to learn directly how inappropriate and ludicrous the children's complaints are. And the therapist needs direct experience with the alienator to observe that parent's manipulations directly. It is only be evaluating all family members, individually and in varying combinations, that one can get a full appreciation of what is going on with the PAS family."* (*The Parental Alienation Syndrome, Second Edition, Richard A. Gardner, MD,© 1992, 1998 by Creative Therapeutics, Inc.)*

And now we have the dubious Dr Rowe taking the stand. Sharply dressed, slick and extremely confident, he rattles off his professional qualifications, and then adds – in an almost supercilious manner – that he has worked in one hundred custody cases and has written one hundred publications. He then dismisses the sexual abuse aspect of the case and proceeds to go over his report. He says the boys' relationship with me should be repaired and that this can be easily achieved.

This is complete rubbish, utter nonsense – he has seen for himself how the boys behaved towards me, their venom and absolute hatred pouring out of their little mouths, as if they were possessed. How can this be 'repaired' at all, let alone 'easily'? As things stand, it would take nothing short of a miracle to get even close to rebuilding the relationship – and it would have to be done with the ever-controlling and interfering JP well out of the way. So much damage has been done, how can this man, this professional expert, be so blasé about the situation? Yet he is. He is so glib, so disinterested in getting to the bottom of the case, he talks about this as if saying a cut finger only needs a sticking plaster. Rowe is never going to admit just how serious this case is.

He now states there is no such thing as PAS. It isn't included in the DSM-IV (this is the Diagnostic and Statistical Manual of Mental Disorders, fourth edition, published in 1994) and so he believes it doesn't exist. He goes so far as to write it off as a 'cottage industry'. He adds that, for the few people who do recognise that PAS exists, the thinking is that children will not behave in an ambivalent fashion towards the victim parent, but they will appear to be 'monolithic' in their attitude. He tells the court that the boys were displaying ambivalence towards me, kissing and hugging me and telling me how much they were missing me.

What? Was he there? Does he not remember the boys screaming at me, their foul language, their physical aggression, having to be restrained? This man really thinks he knows better than any other professional, alive or dead. He doesn't even seem to care that he is advising the court on something so vitally important, so crucial – this is about my children's lives, their future, their mental health and well-being. And I can see now that the court is taking all of this in. This is more madness, just like all of the way through this hellish nightmare.

Richard Gardner wrote his first book on Parental Alienation Syndrome in 1992 and the second edition was published in 1998. Gardner is the accepted expert on PAS and he is recognised as a leading innovator in child psychiatry. His credentials speak for themselves. How can Rowe – the court-appointed 'expert' – not be aware of his work? Here is an excerpt from his 1998 book, 'The Parental Alienation Syndrome, Second Edition': "As was to be expected, *lawyers defending PAS (parents) predictably claimed that the PAS does not exist, especially because it is not yet listed in DSM-IV. Furthermore, some have referred to the PAS as a 'theory' rather than as an actual entity. Primarily it has been judges who have been responsible for the increasing acceptance in the legal literature of PAS. Although some have ruled that it does not exist because there is no scientific 'proof' that it exists, there are other judicial rulings in which it is cited, and the PAS diagnosis is considered a valid one."*

(The Parental Alienation Syndrome, Second Edition, Richard A. Gardner, MD, © 1992, 1998 by Creative Therapeutics Inc.)

Gardner quotes detailed references from which people can check on cases, rulings, legal articles and so on. How can this court not be aware of these cases, these rulings – when they are dealing with a case where PAS is being offered as an explanation for the behaviour of children around whom this case is built?

I stare at Rowe in disbelief. This man, this disgusting individual who purports to be a mental health professional, is repugnant to me. I feel sick and I want to scream and scream until I find myself in a different place where this was all just a bad dream. But I am still here. Rowe has lied so flagrantly, so monstrously – and all under oath.

As I sit, completely shocked at this blatant disregard for honesty, for the law, for his professional standing – he lies yet again! He claims McKay must have forgotten that she did let him have her file on the case, as it was delivered to him by McKay's husband! There is obviously nothing this man will not stoop to, in his determination to avoid the truth.

He dismisses the suggestion that the case could perhaps be a *folie-à-deux* – a shared paranoid delusional syndrome, because, he explains, for this there have to be two delusional people involved. He reminds the court that the only paranoid delusional person in this is Joss.

Suddenly, it hits me – is this the reason why JP's personality test results were mysteriously 'lost'? Would those results perhaps have indicated that JP was, indeed, the other paranoid delusional individual? Rowe is now clearly not just unprofessional and self-opinionated – he is a very dangerous person, I am certain of that.

When asked what he thought about Ryan's report, Rowe – once more totally dismissive – says there is no such thing as PAS and that it is 'ludicrous' for this to even be suggested.

Day one in court is at an end and the judge orders a recess. I am left speechless at Rowe's inflated opinion of himself, of his haughty rejection of anyone else's professional opinions, reports or comments. And then, yet another hail of emotional bullets from the other side – the judge is saying that, should there be snow tomorrow, there will be no court. In fact, if just one person involved can't make it to court because of the weather, the hearing will be cancelled. He adds insult to injury with a feigned attempt at sympathy for us when he adds that he would hate for us to have to travel back here again just to complete the hearing.

He is clearly telling us this is over, finished, and there is no point carrying on with the charade. He has made up his mind, has swallowed every lie, every avoidance of the truth that came out of Rowe's smug mouth. Our testimonies are unimportant, and so is Ryan's. I can't describe how I feel. I just want to curl up and die.

The end of day one . . .

We all went back to Michael's office to discuss what would happen the next day – if, that is, there was no snow. It wasn't snowing at this point, and, even if it did snow, New Mexico was used to it and this shouldn't be an issue.

I wept. I was drained, almost of life itself. Everything I had been fighting for over the past two years, all the money we had poured into this, all of the travelling back and forth, all of the researching, the studying, seeking out people who knew something that might help . . . all of it – useless. All for nothing. Michael and Ryan were trying to get me to see a positive angle, but I knew now there could be none. This was it. Hoffmann was totally on side with the Proctors – he hadn't even bothered to cross-examine them after their testimonies. Rowe was lying at every turn and getting away with it. And now, to illustrate once more the farcical nature of all of this, everything was hanging on whether or not we would have snow.

As that day drew to a close, I knew I was up against a force too powerful to fight. Pure evil.

Day two . . .

In the depths of my immense sense of defeat – because that's what this was, even though no-one had actually spoken the exact words – I had to try, had to summon up all the strength and determination I could muster. I didn't feel strong, nor determined. I felt like I'd been fighting for so long against an increasingly insurmountable enemy, that I had no fight left in me. I felt I had lost. Lost my children, lost my sanity, lost hope and even lost my faith.

And now, just when I have nothing left to fight with, it's my turn to be questioned. All I can do is believe that, in telling the truth as I know it, the court will see what is really going on here. And, with Ryan's professional report and testimony, plus his experience of PAS, surely there has to be some slight chance?

Michael Keene is asking me about the child support arrears, and I tell the court that I had always hoped, once JP finally got his business sorted and properly funded, he would be able to pay what he owed: having lived with him for seven years, I know more than anyone that his finances are, to say the least, unstable. When we were together, he was continually trying to get various businesses off the ground, and when we received that letter from him in 1997, I really believed he had every intention of paying me back. I add that there is also the matter of the eighty thousand dollars which was supposed to help buy a new home for me and the boys, which has never materialised.

> The court didn't want to deal with this particular issue – it was to be treated separately from the custody case, almost as if it were something that couldn't be enforced, even though it was contracted in a legal document.

I describe our house, the boys' schools in the UK, family friends, our lifestyle – including the various sporting activities the boys took part in and enjoyed thoroughly. I speak of the letter JP sent in 1997 and how I have been patient for all of the time since then, waiting for the promises contained in those pages to become reality. I tell the court that, despite the on-going non-payment of child support as ordered by the court, I have never prevented JP from seeing the boys.

Photograph exhibits are being produced – many pictures of the boys as they had been in the UK, each picture telling a very different story from that claimed by the Proctors to be the truth. The children in these photos are smiling, laughing, clean, well dressed – these are pictures of happy children enjoying life.

Now we bring out a tape recording of the telephone conversation between myself and Joss, which – the Proctors claim – caused him to have the fourteen-hour fit because I was 'shouting and screaming' at him down the phone. (We hadn't asked for this tape to be entered as evidence before the hearing and it took the other side by surprise; so much so, JP's lawyer, Burke, tries to have it thrown out. Luckily, the judge allows it.) The tape is played and no-one can argue that this is a mother speaking with affection to her son, asking him what he wanted for his birthday, asking him what he had been doing lately, and sending him her love. It was after this conversation that, according to the Proctors, Joss had the fit and was banging his head against a wall, so that (eventually) he had to be taken to hospital.

I talk about the meeting with the boys at Rowe's office. At first, the boys refused to come out and see me; when they did appear, after twenty minutes, they shouted and swore, using filthy language – nothing they had ever learned at home with us – and they both got into such a state, they had to be restrained.

I try to explain why I had said sorry to Michael. When I had felt so brow-beaten by Rowe and by the way the boys were behaving towards me and Edward, by the way things were looking at the time, Rowe had badgered me into saying it and it was exactly what he wanted so he could use it in court to make me appear guilty. I tell the court this is when the boys had yelled all sorts of accusations at me and Edward – accusations of extremely harsh treatment, physical aggression against them, and even violent beatings. The actual incidents to which they were referring did take place – but only on a normal everyday scale as would happen in most families. Their stories were wildly exaggerated out of all proportion: for example, Michael had been found eavesdropping on a private conversation with a neighbour, and had been told off – scolded, no more than that.

His version of this incident, related in Rowe's office, was a complete fabrication and made it sound as if he had been beaten to within an inch of his life. This type of exaggeration of true events is typical behaviour of children affected by PAS. This was also when the boys had said I was no longer their mother, and Michael stormed out of the room, saying he never wanted to see me again, and adding that he might come and see me when he was eighteen. The whole episode had worn me down so badly, I had no defences left.

Michael asks me why they would have made everything up. I reply that, since the letter of 1997, after which I declined JP's request to have the boys go to live with him, he began drip-feeding them, slowly poisoning them against me at every opportunity. He sold them a fantasy about a new life with him in the States. How wonderful it would be! And he told them not to worry about me because he would fly me out to visit them in the holidays.

Michael asks me, *"How have the last two years been for you?"* and I answer *"Absolute hell."* He adds *"What do you want out of this?"* and I say *"I want my children back – they were my life. This has been torture for me."*

At this point, the judge asked me how I could get the boys back. I explained that this would require some intervention, such as provided by the Rachel Foundation: I outlined the work they carried out, and I told the court that it would entail a one-week residential stay for the boys at the Foundation – and I stressed that I was prepared to pay the costs. The Judge would be able to contact the Foundation every day to monitor progress and, if it failed, then the children would simply return to live with the Proctors. The boys were in such an obvious state of distress, and here was an organisation with a proven track record of working with such cases – surely, this was worth a try?

It's Burke's turn to question me. We go back to when Joss had his febrile seizure at the age of three. I explain that he was taken to hospital and a follow-up letter confirmed that his motor skills were down and his speech was not quite as advanced as it should be. A week later I took him to St George's Hospital in Tooting to have him checked out. He had speech therapy for two months after which he was discharged with a report that he was now well within the accepted range. No further action was advised and so I was satisfied that there was no reason to be concerned – after all, children do develop at different rates.

When asked about Joss' possible psychosis, I reply as firmly as I can, that, if we had been at all worried about this possibility, we would have addressed the issue by taking Joss to the appropriate professionals for advice and, if necessary, treatment. I add that it would have been impossible for other people not to have noticed something if he had been psychotic, and there is nothing in Joss' medical records to suggest anything of the sort. The question has to be asked, as Joss had had three separate visits with the Proctors since 1996, did they not notice anything unusual about his behaviour, and – if they did – why didn't they do something about it while he was in their care? The answer is, there was nothing to notice at that time. Only after being in their care for three months did Joss begin to display symptoms of psychosis.

One of the many allegations is brought up. Michael was supposed to have been beaten over the head with a tennis racquet. The truth is that he fell off an umpire's chair and was taken to hospital straight away. Another allegation is then fired at me – the boys claimed I had failed to collect them from school. Trying to contain my frustration at something so completely mundane being brought up as important in a custody case, I explain that most children in the UK will walk to school with their friends at some point, and certainly don't want their mother tagging along. It's completely ridiculous to make an issue of something so trivial.

On the subject of the tennis 'incident' – one of Michael's accusations at the dreadful meeting in Rowe's office was that he never played tennis, went for walks etc. Why does nobody pick up on all of these anomalies?

I touch on the strange comments from the boys whenever JP would hand them back to me after they had stayed with him, and they appeared distressed and quite antagonistic: at Christmas 1997 the boys told me they were not English any longer, but were American; they asked why I wouldn't let them live in America when it was so much better there. Michael was worse than Joss in this respect and he once cried almost relentlessly, saying he wanted his daddy. But this behaviour would only continue for the first day or so on their return, and soon they would snap out of it and settle back into their normal life with us, with friends and neighbours and so on, and there wouldn't be another word spoken about any of it. Because this phase was only ever short-lived and only happened immediately after a stay in the States, I put it down to the naturally upsetting condition of the boys only having short spells with one parent and the fact that they had just had to say goodbye again for quite a while.

> Even this rather disturbing aspect of the boys' behaviour wasn't really sufficient – at that time – to rush off and seek psychiatric help. If every parent jumped on every tiny thing that didn't fit in with whatever passes for 'normal', and rushed off to get therapy, we would need far more therapists than we have at present.

Why did I not write to the boys? How could I, when they made it very plain they didn't want to have anything to do with me? Then Burke says that the boys did, however, communicate with my mother, which was true. So, how come? This was, in my opinion, manipulation by the Proctors, who had read about PAS and so would know that the condition extends to the whole family of the victim parent. So, to be clever, and make sure PAS could not be proved, they got the boys to write to my mother, who – because she had absolutely no knowledge of PAS – wrote back to them without realising she was playing right into the hands of the Proctors.

This was completely contrived – I knew, beyond any shadow of doubt, as soon as this case was finished with, that contact would end. Again, I would later be proved correct. My mother was totally naïve about this and was simply being a granny who was very happy to hear from her estranged grandsons, and it gave her great pleasure to have contact with them. To illustrate the absolutely 'no-win' aspect of our situation, if she hadn't replied, it could have been said that our family didn't want to have contact with the boys. Damned if you do, damned if you don't.

Burke asks me about the report by Rowe that the boys had been hugging and kissing me, and telling me they missed me, when we met in his office. I almost laugh out loud as I tell the court this is absolutely untrue: they were shouting, swearing, hurling abusive accusations, screaming – and both had to be held back from physically attacking me.

Now it's Hoffmann's turn to cross-examine me. I'm angry that he hasn't even bothered to question the Proctors, but I need to keep my cool. He says that, in 1997, Joss was diagnosed with ADD and was prescribed Ritalin, asking me why didn't Joss have counselling while he was taking this medication? I reply that the doctors looking after Joss never once suggested counselling, otherwise of course I would have done whatever

163

they advised. His tone and attitude are accusatory, and yet how can I be accused of not doing something, when I was not told to do so by the professionals in charge?

He says that what I am suggesting is happening here is evil. The idea of child abduction is abhorrent to anyone – a normal parent could not even contemplate the cruelty of taking a child away from the other parent and poisoning their minds against that parent. Surely I am not accusing the Proctors of being evil? Yes, that's what I'm saying.

He asks how could the Proctors possibly have kept everything secret, if they had this conspiracy against myself and Edward? How could they invent these great fantasies, and how could they manage to fool all of the psychologists except Dr Brand? He quickly follows this up with an almost sympathetic statement, saying how traumatic this must be for me, and asks why haven't I had counselling to help me deal with the loss of my children? I tell him that it is, indeed, very traumatic for me, but I am fortunate to have close friends – one lady in particular – who has spent a lot of time with me, helping me emotionally and also in many practical ways. I tell him my friends are a huge source of support for me.

Once more proving that hindsight is a wonderful quality, I was to learn later, after the hearing, that the judge was a staunch advocate of therapy and counselling: the fact that I had not put myself into therapy was a strike against me. Not getting Joss counselling alongside his medication was another strike. Hoffmann obviously knew this at the time, and used it to put me in a poor light with the judge.

Hoffmann is trying his damnedest to make it appear that I had not taken Joss' condition seriously, and asks me if I am saying the diagnosis of psychosis was incorrect. I manage to fire one back this time, saying *"I find it incredible – he was perfectly OK in the UK and suddenly, when he starts living here, he becomes psychotic!"* I also add that, if Joss had been showing any earlier signs of psychosis, surely the Proctors would have spotted something during the boys' visits.

Things are thrown into the mix that, in my opinion, are totally irrelevant and of no use in the grand scheme, but they all add to build a picture of me and Edward being in the wrong – even a tiny thing like a birthday present arriving two months late, although there was a perfectly adequate explanation for this.

This is all going really badly, I know that. Whatever I say, somehow it ends up going against me. I can see now how court cases can go terribly wrong for the innocent, and how guilty people can get off scot-free. It's all about manipulation, playing to the individual judge – it's a game, and it shouldn't be so.

But – here's one thing to my credit! While Hoffmann is questioning me, I manage to get him to admit that – since he was the only other witness at the time – Rowe was lying about the behaviour of the boys in his office. An audible gasp runs around the courtroom. It's a tiny victory, but it really should carry some weight, to prove that the main professional in this – the court-appointed 706 expert – has lied under oath.

Now, thank heaven, it's Michael who is questioning me. He asks me about the secrets I discovered that the boys were keeping with JP – what did I learn at Christmas 1998? I reply, Michael told me something that he said was a big secret with dad: he said if ever Edward smacked either of the boys, he could go to prison.

I had been shocked and very upset at hearing this and I rang the Proctors right away to discuss it. I just knew there was something very wrong. I was only able to speak to JP's mother-in-law and she refused to talk to me about it; she said JP was away. I told her she must get him to call me as I felt this was very important and we needed to talk about it. He never did.

So, who was it wanted to speak to whom about abuse?

I can't say, to this day, if coming to the end of my time on the stand was more of a relief, because I was in such a state of nerves and felt I might collapse at any time, or if I really wanted to stay there, to keep explaining everything to these people until they realised the truth. There was definitely some relief in getting away from the pressure of the constant questioning – even when you are telling the truth and nothing but the truth. You know that, if you don't say something in exactly the right way, giving your words exactly the right intonation, if you falter before responding, if you so much as blink at the wrong moment – you can be seen to be guilty. It's that easy to get it so very wrong, and yet I would have gladly stayed there for as long as it took, I would have kept going, telling everything over and over to those people, if I thought for one second there was a chance they would begin to understand, to believe me.

A man's voice says it's ten-fifteen and a recess is declared.

It's Edward's turn on the stand and Michael is cross-examining him. Edward confirms that he has been employed in the UK as a firefighter for the past five years and that this means he is on standby for periods of twenty-four hours at a time. On being asked about his other incomes, Edward explains that he has shares in a family business and also has a private property portfolio. Michael asks him about the allegations of excessive alcohol consumption. Edward replies, how on earth could he hold down a fireman's job if he had the dreadful problems with drinking that he and I are being accused of? It would be impossible. He said he wouldn't fancy his chances trying to climb extended ladders or rush into a burning building, while under the influence of alcohol.

Michael asks him to explain about the visa expiration and Edward tells how it is common practice for people to cross over the border to have their visas stamped so they could continue to stay in the area. We both know this isn't seen as a big deal in normal circumstances, but it has been brought up to use as a strike against us.

> At that time, Edward had come over to join me while I was staying in the US for a year, and he was working on a casual basis as a freelance tennis coach in Texas.

Michael asks if Edward had taken part in any activities with the boys when they lived with us. *"Yes, I was a professional tennis player and I taught the boys tennis, taught them to swim, play golf, we walked the dog through the woods together, cycled together . . ."*

Michael asks what about the comments about Edward being undressed around the boys and Edward explains that we were members of a very nice country club, where we took the boys and that entailed them having to get changed with Edward in the men's changing rooms. Up until they were four years old, they got changed with me in the ladies' changing rooms. Michael asks if Edward ever walked into the boys' room naked while they had their friends with them, and Edward replied simply, *"Nonsense."*

When Michael questions Edward about the *"whole lot of talk about the kids being unkempt"*, he says he would refer the court back to the airport incident again – how could their father have possibly left them for a further four days if he had seen them in the dreadful condition he claimed they were in?

When asked about the boys' performance in school, he

replies that they were *"Perfectly normal, above average. If people here had bothered to contact people in England, they would discover there's no evidence of any such problems".*

"Did you encourage them to see their father?" Michael asks, and Edward replies, without hesitation, *"Yes"*, explaining we were aware that, should anything happen to their mother, there was a chance the boys would go back to their father and they therefore need to have a proper relationship with him. *"And who paid for the kids to visit their father?" "I did, on the promise that Mr Proctor would repay this – he never did. Not a very successful businessman."*

"What about the conversations Mr Proctor had with you regarding your disciplining of the kids?" is simple to answer with *"Never happened."* Michael then refers to McKay's reports of *"being kicked up the stairs, hit with a belt buckle, slammed into a wall . . ."* and asks Edward about those accusations. Edward says the kids wouldn't be alive today if that had actually happened.

Michael asks *"How does it strike you that Mr Proctor said the kids were told their primary value was as a source of income from child support?"* Again, Edward is quick and succinct in replying, *"Absolute nonsense. Mr Proctor didn't provide this income – I supported the children."*

Michael ends his cross-examination by asking about the allegations of sexual abuse, to which Edward responds *"Nonsense, all of it. Would we travel four times to the States and spend around a hundred thousand dollars to try to get my wife's children back, and clear my name? I don't take kindly to men on the other side of the Atlantic alleging what Mr Proctor has alleged."* Considering how Edward is feeling, with these dreadful allegations against him, and given that neither of us should even have to be there, let alone trying to defend ourselves when we had done nothing wrong, I think he does an amazing job of being questioned, and this short statement really sums it up.

Then Burke questions Edward and asks why Joss can't swim. This is more utter nonsense – Joss is a very good swimmer, or he was when he lived with us. Anyway, we already covered this subject – does this mean Burke hasn't got anything more useful to ask?

He questions Edward as to where the money came from to pay for the court case, and Edward says – as he mentioned earlier – he sold two properties. Burke tries to suggest that perhaps we received some payment from a media company when we approached them with our story, but Edward doesn't rise to this and simply says *"No."*

Edward says JP is a conman in his business activities and he has now conned his own children.

Now Ryan takes the stand and Michael cross-examines him, beginning with Ryan's credentials, which he details as per his curriculum vitae. Immediately, Bolton objects to Ryan's testimony, arguing that he isn't qualified, and also because PAS isn't listed in the DSM-IV, therefore it doesn't exist.

> The thought flashed through my mind, "Don't tell me they are suddenly going to prevent Ryan giving his testimony, have his report thrown out of court? How can this be happening?"

Ryan explains that he was appointed in April and then he came back in August to see the children. He has to quote several cases in which PAS had been accepted by the courts: there were one hundred and thirty peer review articles and there is currently an application to have PAS included in the forthcoming DSM-V. The judge clears him to continue with his testimony, and his report is discussed – in particular Ryan points out the hallmarks of PAS. He gives examples of the boys exhibiting signs of alienation, such as the hysterical, dramatic scenes; their severely oppositional attitude towards me and Edward as displayed in Rowe's office; the overtly dramatic behaviour in front of the judge at the Hague Convention hearing.

Ryan tells the court that the Achenbach Checklist used by McKay could not possibly be carried out in a two-week period.

Then he states categorically that this is a legal parental abduction of children.

Michael quickly repeated the phrase, but used the word 'alienation' instead of 'abduction'. In their preparations for the hearing, Michael had advised Ryan not to use the term 'abduction' as it is such a revolting idea and he thought using such would not help to get people on side. But poor Ryan had seen this before and was so incensed by it, he just couldn't help himself when he was in full flow on the stand.

Ryan's report was excellent – truly professional, clearly informative and thorough, and it clearly showed his extensive expertise on the subject of parental alienation.

In the report, Ryan expresses his immediate concerns as: ". . . child endangerment issues need to be addressed. The Proctor boys have suffered from severe psychological disturbances while in the custody of their father. Joss in particular is vulnerable and at a high risk to compromising his physical safety and has the potential of acting out by making a suicide gesture.

In my opinion, Joss has been misdiagnosed because of a fabricated history given by his father, Mr Proctor. This misdiagnosis has resulted in the prescription of drugs that are inappropriate. According to school personnel, Joss is developing a speech disorder and exhibiting other symptoms, which, in my opinion, are probably an iatrogenic effect and neurological impairment from taking toxic medication. The debilitating symptoms of impairment that Joss is exhibiting are described *in the clinical psychotropic drug manual as adverse side effects, especially when combining two of the medications he has been taking. Joss' judgment is severely impaired and he is impulsive."*

He adds that, because the Proctors were so 'highly invested' in presenting the boys as being 'sick' and 'damaged' by myself and Edward, they were not helping the boys and were actually endangering them even further.

> The report documents the point when it first became clear that JP wanted to gain custody, and quotes from the letter he had sent to me, Edward and the boys back in August 1997: *"Finally, most importantly I wanted my boys . . . I want my boys to come and live with us for a while . . . I am their Father and I think we need to be together"* and so on.
>
> The accusations are listed in the report, including the glaring anomaly: *"In addition to accusing Pamela of being an alcoholic, she was accused of taking Joss' Ritalin because of drug dependence, at the same time being accused of overdosing and overmedicating Joss with the same medication."*

It was so good to hear someone actually picking up on all of this and showing it for the nonsense it was – and it was all there, in black and white, written by someone who knew what he was talking about, someone who saw the truth of the situation. I was pinning a lot of hope on this report. It stated that the Proctors were exploiting Joss and Michael in order to win custody by fabricating allegations of abuse, and that the boys had been *"positioned to convince people in authority that they led a life of 'off-the-charts' chronic severe abuse and deprivation at the hands of their mother and stepfather. Joss and Michael began their participation after they were with their father and stepmother for a month."* It went on to point out that the boys didn't make any allegations of sexual abuse at the beginning, but only after they had been living with the Proctors for a while.

On the subject of Dr McKay, she who had set this dreadful machine in operation by her report right at the start, Ryan opines *"Dr McKay was blind sighted and did not detect John's [Proctor's] agenda. John brought Joss and Michael forward to see Dr McKay when he had enough confidence that Joss and Michael would pass the 'loyalty' test.*

In my opinion, Dr McKay's conclusions had a significant influence on a chain of service providers resulting in misinterpretations leading to misdiagnoses and improper treatment of the Proctor boys. The escalation in severe psychological symptoms exhibited by the Proctor boys, especially Joss, were not seen as iatrogenic disorders caused by the wrong treatment in the context of severely alienated children. Instead, the behaviour was interpreted as confirmation of the allegations of abuse, though Dr McKay never met with mother and stepfather."

Ryan then stated his opinion that JP co-opted McKay to say that the boys were abused children and to recommend that temporary custody be granted to JP. Commenting on her claim that the situation was *"consistent with abuse"*, he said this claim was without foundation, adding *"In general, psychologists are warned of the potential danger in causing harm when manoeuvring from clinical to forensic roles by making recommendations in a custody dispute without evaluating all the parties."*

Sound professional advice of the highest order – which McKay, most unfortunately, did not follow.

Giving dates and individuals for reference, the report covered the deterioration in the condition of the boys up to September 2000, by which time Joss – being the more vulnerable of the two – was exhibiting *"some of the most severe psychological dysfunction any of the service providers, including school personnel, have ever seen."* It also noted that, in March 2000, McKay had recommended hospitalisation, saying she considered Joss to be 'gravely disabled' – the Proctors never acted on this recommendation.

Ryan's medical findings included Joss being diagnosed with Attention Deficit Disorder (ADD) in 1998 in the UK and that he was prescribed Ritalin and was monitored by Dr B L Lee who reported 'significant progress' while on this medication. The Ritalin was taken away from Joss shortly after he began living with the Proctors and Ryan reports this as *"Absent medication that was helping Joss to function probably exacerbated an already next to impossible situation for Joss to adjust to."*

There is so much more in Ryan's report – all very crucial to the case, including him listing those professionals who, in his opinion, had *"misdiagnosed the case and made incorrect recommendations to change custody as well as place the Proctor boys in the wrong treatment."* Also noted specifically is Dr Rowe, for failing to produce the two psychological tests that JP was supposed to have taken, and that Rowe had said he based his recommendations on the information and records supplied to him by McKay – and yet she put in writing *"Dr Rowe did not speak with me nor review records regarding my treatment of these boys."* Rowe's input in the case is noted in the report as erroneous and damaging, plus he was obstructive to Ryan by not returning calls and so on.

Dr Gomez is also given the spotlight in the report: *"Dr Gomez was consciously deceptive . . . Sent me to an office location that he completely vacated the previous day . . . [I] gave him the court order allowing me to examine records and confer and tried to get him to return my call, which he never did".*

This entire case, from start to finish, was populated by 'professionals' who would side with the Proctors – the alienating party – without so much as an interview or even a simple telephone conversation with me – the mother of the children, the victimised parent and the parent with rights of custody.

A lady called Abigail Hunter had her twelve-year-old son abducted by his father while on a visit to the US in 2007. In her story of her own experiences with PAS, she says *". . . without meeting me or contacting me, the psychologist began what became an irreversible process by advising the lawyers acting for both sides that, as my son had an apparent fear of me, access – if any – should be short and supervised. Accordingly, I saw Joe for an hour and a quarter in a café. His father stayed by the exit, within earshot, on guard.*

I'd give my life to protect my son, yet here he was being 'protected' from the fabricated danger that I represented."

Basically, Ryan's report covered every aspect of the case, and his findings were that there was no evidence for any of the allegations. What we found very interesting was that he went on to say *"if even some of the Proctors' allegations represent projections, then alcohol along with some of the other content issues may be significant in the Proctor home. The accusation that the Roches only care about money and not their children may be a projection of a possible motivating factor that drives the Proctors."*

As well as the fact that Ryan had assessed the boys against the twelve criteria used in diagnosing parental alienation and they both matched all twelve points, he included in the report the reasons quoted as to why parents alienate children. One of these is money. It shouldn't have escaped anyone involved that JP began this grotesque charade at a point when he owed me a very substantial amount of unpaid child support.

The report recommends some intervention by the Rachel Foundation, that custody be granted to me so that the boys can come back to live in the UK with us, and that – before any decisions are made as to future involvement with the Proctors – JP and Tess undergo a psychological or psychiatric evaluation.

A recess is called and Judge McDougall says he wants to see the children. My heart pounds at hearing this – how will they behave? Will they be the same as they were with the judge at the Hague Convention hearing? Will their behaviour allow the judge to see that they are brainwashed? Or will he believe them if they shout and scream about the 'abuse' we are supposed to have put them through? The recess is short but it seems like hours, waiting to see what happens next.

The judge reappears and speaks to the lawyers; Michael walks over to us and tells us the judge said he can't send the boys back to the UK. That's it. All over.

Ryan continues; he produces the Rachel Foundation information pack, which is handed round. Once more, Burke tries to have this rejected. Ryan tries to explain the work of the Foundation and how they have improved the standard of this specialised support service: previously, children would have to be seen in a hotel room for such sessions, but the Foundation offers residential care. This is vital, as the children need to be stabilised and taken away from the Proctors for a while so the intervention can be more effective.

Burke chips in again. He has noticed Ryan's name and also

Ryan's wife's name on the Rachel Foundation folder, and he queries whether Ryan is receiving any fee from them, and whether the Foundation is federally funded. (Ryan's wife was a renowned forensic psychologist who specialised in parental alienation, parental abduction, and other forms of complex psychological abuse.) Ryan is a member of the Board of Directors of the Rachel Foundation and Burke is using this against him, suggesting he is biased and has a vested interest in recommending the Foundation.

Mention is made of the *American Standard Custody Evaluation Guidelines.* These guidelines are for the assessment of three aspects essential when considering custody: the parental capacity of the parents; the psychological needs of the children; and the resulting fit between parents and children. Ryan's report states that our parental capacity was shown to be good, whereas the Proctors didn't correspond to the psychological needs of the boys. What did emerge from their evaluation was severe psychological and emotional abuse.

When asked if he had examined Rowe's testing data, and what was his assessment of this, Ryan says he wasn't able to examine the data, and therefore wasn't able to form any assessment, because two significant tests were missing from the batch. These were JP's MMP12 and TAT test results, and no-one seemed to have any idea where these were. *"Are any of the children's parents delusional?" "I don't know because JP's tests are missing. But the children's primary condition is a pathological attachment to their father."*

Answering whether or not he considered Dr Rowe had done 'a good job', Ryan replies that Rowe did a good job in relation to an everyday, run-of-the-mill custody case, but that Rowe simply didn't see the bigger picture.

Both Burke and Hoffmann play heavily on the question of two small children being able to keep a secret for a whole year, since JP had apparently planted the idea in their minds about going to live with him in the States, and ask Ryan if he thinks it feasible that they could carry on living with us for all of that time and never once let anything slip. How easy it is for these people to twist things.

Even with Ryan's report and testimony, I can see most people in the courtroom are thinking the same things and we have little or no credibility.

A recess is announced and we are to reconvene at a quarter to five.

I simply couldn't be in that room, with the Proctors, and with Hoffmann, Burke and everyone else who thought Edward and I were guilty – even though some of them weren't at all sure what it was we were supposed to have done – and I couldn't give them the satisfaction of seeing me break down when the judge announced his findings. I was already shaking, falling apart. I told Michael we had to go and he asked the judge if that would be OK: he said yes and we walked with our arms around each other, out into the cold air, to the icy car park which seemed to represent my life – always unsure of stepping anywhere in case of another fall, always feeling tentative and threatened by something causing my downfall, trying desperately to keep my footing. The day was drawing to a close and the moon was casting its eerie silver light behind the Sandia mountain range that towered over us – just as the awful court case had overshadowed our lives. We got into our car and sat quietly, away from that austere room and those people so full of lies and deceit. It felt safer there.

People are coming out of the building . . . it must be over now. We see Michael and his business partner, looking so professional in their dark suits and black overcoats, and we get out of the car to speak with them. They tell us what has been decided – we already knew without hearing the words. They tried to win the case for us, but they lost, and it's clear from their faces that they feel bad. Especially Michael, as I believe he really was fighting for us, for the boys. Without thinking, I give them both a hug – I'm brimming with so many emotions . . .

Later, when we had the tapes of the court hearing, we listened to the closing statements, some of which made us feel a little more positive and some made us feel worse. But, overall, we had still lost the case and lost the boys.

Hoffman was first to give his closing statement.

"I think this case is a tragedy . . . there are no winners . . . I think the Proctors need to hear this. The kids should stay here . . . I really don't think that taking them out of their existing home and placing them somewhere like the Rachel Foundation – which I have questions about – then sending them over to England . . . that doesn't make sense.

I think the situation just snowballed . . . The kids said things and the Proctors just believed them. They didn't say 'maybe that's not true' or 'you still need to have a relationship with your mother' and they should have done that.

I don't think the Roches or the Proctors are bad people but the situation took on a life of its own. What really happened, none of us will ever know.

I think there should be one over-riding psychologist who works with both parents and children . . . I don't think Joss has seen a psychiatrist in a while and he needs to see someone. But I would rather Joss see a psychologist who has experience of high-conflict cases, parental alienation and all of this stuff that's been raised here.

We need to see what we can do to try to give these kids

more of a normal life. We need to make arrangements for Mrs
Roche to visit – this will cost a lot of money and probably what
we'll hear is 'I don't have it' . . ."

Then it was Burke's turn.

"When the boys came over in 1999, John Proctor saw
something worse than he had seen before. The boys reported
a level of abuse that they had not reported before.

This goes back to 1996, 1997. In 1997 he first suspected
something – he didn't know what. He spoke to the mother and
the mother gave him assurances.

I think John acted responsibly and tried to contact all of the
state agencies . . .

. . . not clear why the English authorities weren't contacted
. . . Dr McKay testified and said she tried and couldn't get
through, for reasons we don't know . . . the delay of more than
a year after Dr Rowe's report was caused by the mother because
she wanted a second opinion – not by my client.

They hired their 'hired gun' and he came up with the theory
of parental alienation and shared . . . delusion . . . whatever it's
called.

When we check the list of Rachel Foundation advisors, there
are one, two, three . . . six people listed who are persons who
Dr Brand cites as his authorities in his literature and evaluation.
I think he's pursuing an agenda."

(Michael made an objection to this comment.)

"Mr Proctor made a mistake with the child support. He should
have gone to his Texas divorce lawyer when his business went
south and had the child support agreement modified. That was
a mistake.

We ask that the court follow Dr Rowe's recommendations
and that there be a further hearing on finances.

Thank you."

Michael's turn.

"This case started with a Temporary Restraining Order, based on a litany of allegations.

We have heard from a lot of people, a lot of experts.

Dr Rowe's memory of events, to say the least, is spotty.

Dr McKay made a recommendation that the boys remain here . . . then, after three months of treating the boys, realised maybe these allegations weren't true and the older boy might be psychotic, and then Mr Proctor comes back to court and raises further accusations – of sexual abuse . . .

Dr Ryan Brand has spent a considerable amount of time on this case, far more than anybody else. He's the only person to interview collateral witnesses in England – he spent a lot of time contacting the relevant people in England – where all these allegations that led to the temporary restraining order in the first place were purported to occur. Nobody else has any independent verification from anyone in England, no-one else ever contacted anybody in England.

Your Honour, my client is purporting that there is Parental Alienation Syndrome; there is ample evidence to support that. You heard Mrs Roche testify that, on more than one occasion, the children came back and were acting strangely, saying things they had never said before, acting in ways they had never acted before.

You know, they told friends in England that they wouldn't be coming back in 1999?

They accosted their mother in Dr Rowe's office. It took them twenty minutes before they would even talk to her. There was no ambivalence, Your Honour: everyone agrees that in a parental alienation syndrome there has to be no ambivalence, and there was none. Dr Rowe was just wrong.

Your Honour, we saw the children in chambers earlier. Joss was mellow, but that could be a result of the medication. But he immediately blurts out "We don't want to go back!" Michael burst into tears. Joss has not got one good thing to say about England. Then, after some promptings, Michael says, well, the golf is OK, and the tennis is OK . . .

We have a series of outlandish allegations raised by my client . . . let's just look at a couple of little things that happened. The children arrive in Houston and their hair hasn't been combed, and Mr Proctor does his ritual . . . which is to take them to the barber shop to get their hair cut and washed and combed and styled. Then, a couple of days later, they arrive in New Mexico where their stepmother says their hair hasn't been combed! Somebody's not telling the truth . . .

Parental alienation aside . . . Why don't we look at which parent is in a better position to care for these children? We have the father, who's testified he has no income except money from loans, he works from seven a.m. to nine p.m. on most days, six to seven days a week, and has a child support arrearage of over a hundred and twenty-five thousand dollars. He's not even involved in the raising of the children – he's not their primary care-giver. He's not there! They are with their stepmother.

And then we have their mother, who raised them for ten years as a stay-at-home mom. This is what she did her whole life, she raised her children. And then they were taken away.

Mr Burke says this doesn't have to be a zero-sum game. Then, how come, after a phone call, which was played in court today, did they come running back to you again, saying you have to suspend telephonic visitation – Joss is having a fit again? Sounds like a zero-sum game.

With respect to who should pay for visitation, Mr Proctor may have made a mistake in not getting his child support reduced – that's not our problem and he owes that money, and he owes that money whether he pays for this visitation or not. He shouldn't be rewarded in this case because of mistakes in an earlier case. And, should the Roches pursue that child support, it's pretty obvious what's going to happen.

Your Honour, we ask that you return the children to the Roches, however that is feasible.

Thank you."

And, finally, the judge sums up.

"My ruling will be brief. This case bothers me.

It would not be in the best interests of the children to have them removed from the Proctors' home and returned to England.

There are a lot of aspects of this case that bother me, and Mr Hoffmann articulated my feelings, probably better than I can but I will attempt to do so.

My first concern is that I don't think this case fits parental alienation. We have a missing father, Mr Proctor, who, in 1996 begins to have some contact with his children, and, from 1996 to December 1999, he had very little contact except for some brief times during Christmas and one time during the summer of 1999. I find it difficult . . . I find it almost impossible to believe that he could exert the kind of influence upon these children that would be necessary for them to carry forward this conspiracy to continue to insist that they were abused.

So, that having been said, in 1999 I don't believe that these children were the subject, or were being alienated from the other parents. However, based on what took place in my office, the testimony from Dr Brand and the evidence that I have had in this case, I think there has been a continuing attempt, or at least a continuing campaign, to limit access for Mrs Roche and, in that sense, this is an alienation case. Since Mr Proctor has had the children in January 2000, their animosity towards their mother has increased and I blame the Proctors.

They have not dealt with this case in the way I would have hoped they would.

This case is a train wreck that started in 1997 – there were indications from both sides that things were happening with these children and no-one took action. The Proctors didn't contact the child protection services in England.

I think Mrs Roche should have access to these children – she needs to develop a relationship with the children.

She will be given telephonic access and the conversations will be tape recorded, both in England and in the United States.

She will be given supervised visits if she so desires. It is my inclination that Mr Proctor should pay for her to come to the United States . . . somebody needs to come up with a plan to reunite these children with their mother.

I reject completely that Mr Proctor made a mistake . . . when you have an obligation to support your children, you have an obligation to give them something, anything you can give . . . if you can't give them nine hundred dollars, then give them one hundred dollars, or two hundred dollars. To say it was OK for him not to pay is not something I will accept and will not tolerate.

I have concerns about Joss and the type of therapy that he's been receiving and the fact that he's not receiving any treatment. Joss should be seen by a psychiatrist and I am going to require that. Mr Hoffmann, who do you recommend?"

Hoffmann replies that this needs to be someone in Santa Fe and he has no contacts there. He says he will try to find a child psychiatrist in the Santa Fe area.

JP chipped in at this point, telling the judge that Joss was actually seeing Dr Gomez once a month, and stressing how difficult and lengthy the process of finding someone had been – he said Gomez was the 'only one' who could possibly work with Joss. Tess added that all Gomez did was dispense Joss' medications and nothing else. She said they had tried to talk to him but to no avail. The judge cut her short and made it clear that he wasn't at all happy with the current situation – as he put it, "fifteen minutes of 'how are you doing, Joss?' and then handing out yet more medication" was not enough and this was all the more reason to find someone else.

The judge continues: *"And all of the testing must be made available to the psychiatrist.*

I want to see a treatment plan for this child. I want this child to be seen by someone. I want a recommendation with regard to treatment and the type of treatment he should receive.

Mr Keene, on behalf of the Roches – I know they're not here – how do you wish to proceed with regard to access with the children and for your client to re-establish her relationship with the children? Do you want a subsequent hearing?"

Michael replied that that might be appropriate, and asked if he could get back to the court in due course, which the judge agreed to.

"I will require the parties to submit findings and conclusions within ten days;

Mr Keene, would you like to prepare an interim order which sets out your client's right to visitation and telephone contact with the children?

Something happened in England – I don't believe it was a normal life.

Like Mr Hoffmann, the things the children have said to me in my chambers have disturbed me. I have dealt with many high-conflict divorce cases but I have never seen that before, when the first thing out of the boy's mouth was 'I don't want to go back!' – I didn't even have time to introduce myself! That disturbs me and suggests that something else is going on.

The Proctors will begin to attempt to encourage their children to have a healthy relationship with their mother. The terms of the Order will be as normal and will include that no party shall speak negatively about the other party in the presence of the children.

If the Proctors had contacted the child protection services in England, there would have been an investigation and we would have some documentation.

Something else is going on and I am going to require that it stop.

Mr Keene, I would like you to convey to your clients that some of the allegations, especially the sexual abuse allegations, based on Dr Rowe's testimony I can completely discount. I make this decision specifically for the sake of the children, no other reason."

There was mention of fees and the judge said that we should contribute towards Hoffmann's costs.

Still addressing Michael, the judge went on *"I want from you a brief Order that changes custody – call it a Temporary Order. We need a document that establishes your client's ability to have access to the children.*

I suppose there has to be a Child Support Order? Given the arrearages that Mr Proctor owes in this case, that should be part of any child support order."

He then asked if there was anything else to be covered and Michael answered simply, *"No."*

The judge then declared a recess and that's where the tape recording ends.

We make our way back to the Hotel La Posada in miserable silence. What could either of us say that would make this any easier to bear? Set in downtown Albuquerque, the hotel has a beautiful old timbered bar where someone is playing the piano softly, giving the place an inviting atmosphere. The building is full of character, with vibrant etchings depicting Native American Indian culture adorning the walls. Such lovely surroundings to enjoy, but I am so numb, so drained, I could have been anywhere on the planet and hardly noticed a thing. I just sit, looking down at the table, drinking my wine in the hope that it, at least, will help me sleep later.

Post mortem . . .

Ryan came and joined us for an evening drink and I couldn't hold back my tears as we went over the events of the two days in court. Poor Ryan apologised to us, saying he felt it was his fault we had lost, that he should have done better, tried harder. I told him, quite genuinely, that this wasn't down to him at all. For some reason I've never yet worked out, it wouldn't have mattered who or what we had on our side, we would have lost. The court would not listen to any of our evidence – real evidence from real people who knew what they were talking about; but they did take in everything JP said, every disgusting lie that slithered from that evil mouth – without a shred of proof of any kind, without witnesses, without documents, records, and with a testimony that a first-year law student should have been able to tear apart.

So many thoughts . . .
My brain is crammed with questions, disbelief, attempts to understand . . . and yet nothing ever makes sense.

Why is it that none of the so-called 'professionals' – supposedly earning their not inconsiderable fees by taking part in the attempts to resolve this case – can see beyond the very surface of what is right in front of them? Why do they all seem to refuse to look further? It's not the fact that the boys are lying about things, denying their real past life, fabricating wild stories of violence, neglect and abuse, and everything else they have thrown at us – you have to ask *why is this happening?* Where is all this coming from? Why are two young children doing this?

Then there are the sexual abuse allegations – God knows, this has almost driven poor Edward to the brink, given that he is completely innocent of any such thing. Because Rowe has now said these accusations cannot be proven – what? We all pretend they were never made? NO! We have to ask where these two little boys got all of this from – the adult language, the details. This has had to come from somewhere else – children cannot conjure this kind of thing out of thin air! And yet, these 'professionals' are happy to sweep *this very important aspect* of the case under the legal carpet.

And all of this excessively antagonistic, oppositional

behaviour by the children towards us. This is NOT normal in abuse cases. We have documented evidence to support our claims that their behaviour is in line with children who have been alienated. Why are these people so keen to simply accept that this behaviour is the result of the former 'abuse' of which we are so wrongly accused? And why is no-one asking why the boys are not showing signs of improving, when we have had no input or influence in their lives for some time now? This is something that *needs to be investigated further.* And yet, no further interest. End of.

My main question – above and beyond all the millions of others in my head – is why, oh why, do these people, who are supposed to be educated, intelligent, intellectual, qualified, experienced . . . why do they swallow every word JP says, when he has NO proof, NO witnesses, NO evidence, NO knowledge, NO credibility, NOTHING. By the same token, we have proof, documents, witnesses, testimonials, medical records, school records, personal references, and a boat-load of evidence about PAS – and they won't listen to a word we say.

What is really going on here? Will I ever know the truth? This is all so very wrong.

Ryan fills us in on what the judge had said after we left the courtroom. I'm barely listening to him but, suddenly, he says something that changes my mood: the judge had ordered that Joss should see a new psychiatrist in Santa Fe, to 'get to the bottom of what was wrong with him'. JP, of course, had objected on the grounds that his medical insurance wouldn't cover such work, but Judge MacDougall insisted, saying this must take place in Santa Fe – and that JP must pay for it.

One tiny, almost imperceptible, scrap of justice.

In my hopeless state of mind, I cling to this new information. Here would be someone else to become involved, someone new, someone not caught up in what had gone before, someone who could review the UK medical records, work it all out, see what was really going on in this terrible case. If this person were even halfway to being professional, they would surely want to speak to me as well. They would need to see Rowe's report and also Ryan's report, they would see Ryan's very professional handling of things, they would realise he has much experience of this type of case . . . my head is racing way into the future, building on this one glimmer of hope for the truth to finally emerge.

Out of the depths . . .

Later, in our room, Edward and I sat and ate the biggest burrito we had ever seen, bought from a fast food stand outside the hotel. I was crying non-stop but at least I was getting some food into myself. For the past few days my stomach had been so bad in my state of nervous tension and stress, I hadn't eaten at all and I was beginning to feel quite poorly – hardly surprising.

As we sat there, I was suddenly filled with an overwhelming anger. My children had been stolen from me – there really is no other word for it – by a man who had hardly anything to do with them. I was the one who'd gone through the sleepless nights and everything that goes with having two babies and no support from a partner; I was the one who had taken all responsibility for their education, health matters, homework, taking them to various sporting and social events – being completely tied as people are with toddlers. I was the one filling weekends with things to amuse, entertain and help them develop. As any parent will no doubt agree, unless you are wealthy and can pay for nannies and other support, you give up your own life to accommodate theirs. I did it all without even a scrap of financial support from the person who then took them, once I had done all of the hard work.

My new-found anger took on a life of its own and started to make me feel stronger again.

It was at this point that I knew I wanted to have another child. I was now forty and Edward was forty-nine but it was still a possibility for us. I was not going to allow this unbelievable tragedy destroy my chance of having a family life; we already had dear little Dani but I just knew I had to have another baby, a sister or brother for her. Perhaps this would be my healing process, who knows? That sounds very wrong, I know, but – unless you have lost a child – you can't really say how you would feel about this. I may have lost my boys but that didn't mean I had to live without a complete family. My decision was made.

We flew back to the UK again, to yet another bleak January day. Drained, defeated, physically weak – the best description I can come up with is that I felt wounded and I knew I needed to heal, to recover and regain my strength.

So – back home to face life without my boys, to pick up the pieces that were left after this vast, enormous thing had taken over my entire life for the past two years. Thank God for little Dani, and for my dearest Edward, who has been through his own hell because of this. Some alienated parents who lose their child or children never have any more – how on earth do they go on?

Edward and I were never big on using e-mail, but the court case had naturally meant lots of electronic communications going back and forth for so long now. That little red light on the computer, telling us we had mail, was on far more than it was off. And now, there was no little red light. It was over.

I did have a last e-mail from Michael Keene saying there was quite a bit of 'mopping up' to be done now the case was finished, and he very kindly offered to do this work free of charge. How I hated that phrase, 'mopping up', because it made it all seem so finished, done with, something to be cleared away and forgotten.

Ryan sent me a lovely last message of his own, telling me he would never forget me or the case. It was very touching. He said he was going to carry on with the matter of reporting to the Board on the ethical misconduct of McKay, Rowe and Gomez. I thanked him and wished him well.

Even amongst all of this finality, I still had the last little hope that the new psychiatrist would come to the rescue: so many professionals had not done their jobs properly – surely it was time for this to change?

The final order from the custody case came next, consisting of a couple of pages of rulings. I was to be allowed visitation, but not Edward at that time; I was to be allowed telephone contact with the boys and all such conversations were to be recorded by both parties; any visits I made would be supervised and I must give four weeks' notice so that Hoffmann, the children's lawyer, would review the 'proposed visitation plan' and either approve this or would work with me to form a 'more appropriate plan'.

Item five of this order announced that *"Joss Proctor shall undergo treatment and counselling by a suitable psychiatrist and psychologist. All medical and psychological records of Joss Proctor shall be made available to the treating psychiatrist and psychologist".*

And the order concludes with item six: *"Each party will be supportive of each child's relationship with the other parent and neither party, nor their friends or relatives, will intentionally align any child against the other parent or the other parent's family".*

Anyone who had witnessed all that had gone before in this case, JP's blatant lying and cover-ups, his glaring discrepancies of testimony, his vile accusations which were never proved by even the most remote scrap of evidence, and his sickeningly sanctimonious attitude to those who mattered – anyone would know, without a doubt, that this was not worth the paper it was written on because it would *never* happen. Not in the Proctor's camp, not in a million years.

And, of course, the never-ending financial slap in the face for me – the fees of the GAL, Hoffmann, *"shall be divided equally between the parties".*

Chapter twenty-one

aftermath

As a follow-up from the custody case, Hoffmann, being the children's GAL, had to advise where to go next in terms of the boys' issues. He sent a letter to Michael Keene and to Burke dated the thirteenth of March, 2002, posting a copy to the Proctors and faxing the same to me in England.

His first recommendation was that Joss should carry on seeing Deena Thomas, PhD, who was a licensed clinical psychologist, for therapy at his school. She was, apparently, experienced in high-conflict custody cases and Hoffmann said he believed she had established a 'good rapport' with Joss and that he was confident with her.

Next recommendation was that someone called Carol Kerr, PhD, was willing to see Michael for therapy and also to work with the adults – this group included the Proctors, Edward and myself – 'in whatever way is necessary'. This would be something else I would be expected to pay for, even if that was to be fifty-fifty with JP.

He also recommended an updated psychiatric evaluation of Joss. Given that Rowe diagnosed childhood psychosis, Thomas believed it to be Asperger Syndrome, and Gomez recently advised the Proctors that Joss was suffering from Post Traumatic Stress Disorder, it was clear to even a non-professional that

Joss needed to be re-evaluated and his medication needed to be checked to ensure he was taking the correct dosage – and the correct drugs.

Dr Thomas had put forward William Jones, MD, to take on the new psychiatrist's role, but there was an opportunity for Carol Kerr to recommend an alternative. Hoffmann would decide who this would be and he said he wanted *"the new psychiatrist to be experienced and competent and willing to work and communicate with Dr Thomas and Dr Kerr"* as well as to communicate with Hoffmann himself. I would have thought 'experienced and competent' should really be taken as read, but perhaps he was learning from what had transpired so far in this case, and not taking anything for granted.

His letter concludes by asking Michael Keene and Burke to *quickly* discuss these points with *"your respective clients"* and get back to him so that they could move forward with *"this plan as expeditiously as possible"*.

Something told me he had realised the boys need to be provided with the correct support without any further delay. Pity no-one had considered this earlier.

I remember reading in Richard Gardner's book that, in a lot of the PAS cases he had known, when the judge didn't know how to deal with the case, they would simply hand it over to the therapists for them to sort out. The problem here is that the therapists could go ahead and provide endless sessions of therapy but the child is in the wrong place to be able to receive therapy: the child cannot improve because the source of the problem is in the alienator's household, where the child still lives and is still subject to all of the influences and controls. In fact, having sessions of therapy and continuing to live amid the turmoil and unrest could cause total confusion in the child, thereby making things worse, rather than better.

Alienators don't know how to stop what they have started. They don't realise the damage they are causing to the child and the whole scenario is way over the heads of many therapists who have no real relevant experience. It can be incredibly convincing when listening to children screaming and shouting that they have been hurt, mistreated, abused. It is certainly not an easy thing, to search beyond the obvious when it is something so blatant. Add to this, if the alienator is of a psychopathic nature, they have no guilt, remorse or empathy towards their victims. Some children even threaten to commit suicide if they are returned to the alienated parent – imagine being the therapist who dares to hand the child over to the alienated parent. If you get it wrong, the potential consequences don't bear thinking about.

So, in this case, the judge had done exactly what most other judges would have done.

Over the next weeks and months, there were many telephone calls from me to Hoffmann, complaining to him that it was taking too long to arrange a consultation. After all, he had been the one expressing the need to expedite matters. I found out on the twenty-seventh of May that the Proctors had cancelled an appointment made for Joss to see Dr Jones on the eleventh of June, and – completely out of the blue – they had suddenly booked a holiday from the tenth of June until the twenty-sixth of June, rescheduling Joss' appointment to the twenty-fifth of July.

This meant a further delay of six more weeks and was totally unacceptable. I had no choice but to write a letter to Hoffmann, with a copy going to the judge: my letter was dated the sixth of June. It advised that I had had a conversation with the school therapist, Deena Thomas, two days previously and that she agreed with me completely that this is urgent, and she said she would call Hoffmann to discuss the matter. I wrote *"My son is seriously ill and needs psychiatric care. Did the judge intend for this court order to take 7 months to happen when he gave this ruling in January? I tried to call you last week about this issue but you didn't return my calls."*

I added, to give Hoffmann a bit of a scare, that I was intending to travel out in July for my court appointed supervised visit to meet the boys and Dr Jones. I knew this was something he wouldn't want to happen.

Eventually, after the Proctors had prevaricated for seven months, Joss was taken to see Dr Jones – not by his father, nor even his stepmother. He was accompanied to this appointment by his eighty-two year old grandmother; this was no doubt an attempt to play down the importance of the meeting. On top of this, Dr Jones was misled completely as to the reason he had been asked to see Joss: he believed this to be a one-off consultation to review Joss' medications.

The report written by Dr Jones after this meeting was yet another travesty in this ever-lengthening line of travesties. He had simply taken everything the Proctors had told him and accepted every word of it as hard fact, which he then built into his report. I could barely contain my anger as I read it:

"Following the parents' divorce, Joss & his brother Michael were cared for by their mother & stepfather & were taken to England by them. It became clear to the boys' Dad that they were being physically & mentally abused & neglected, so he sued for custody & won. Mom apparently disputed the custody award & her exclusion from seeing the boys except in supervised settings, so she has raised the issue of parental alienation syndrome & 'brainwashing'. The court did ask that a child psychiatrist review Dr Gomez's care & determine if overmedication was occurring."

Firstly, no physical, mental or any other form of abuse had been proven to any degree, so these allegations should *not* have formed any part of this report. Secondly, the purpose of Dr Jones seeing Joss was in order that a complete psychiatric re-evaluation could be carried out over a period of time – nothing to do with *"the estranged mother's concerns that her son is being overly medicated in order to 'brainwash' him."*

"When the grandparents got re-involved about 3 years ago, Joss was functioning very poorly. He was not toilet trained . . . He was far below grade level in school."

How much proof did I have to produce to assure people that Joss *was* completely normal in his toilet habits? If those concerned had ever bothered to gather any of my evidence, they would know from family, our GP, the hospital, the teachers and the school, our neighbours, friends . . . anyone and everyone even remotely involved with our lives, that this was a complete and utter lie on the part of the Proctors. His behaviour and academic progress were also demonstrably normal for his age. We had witnesses who were – and still are – prepared to give evidence of all of these things but no-one ever wanted to listen.

Paragraph five of this work of fiction is an absolute hoot: *"The grandparents had responded to their son & daughter-in-laws pleas for help in managing the kids by moving out to NM from Houston, where they'd retired after service in the U.N."*

Not in any universe, in any lifetime, did JP's parents work for the UN!! This shows how you can say anything – no matter how ridiculous, how far from the truth, how totally insane – and these people, for some reason, will not, do not, *ever* bother to check on anything.

"Joss used to be close to his MGMo (maternal grandmother), Brenda, but she is not allowed to talk to them any more."

Meaning we weren't allowing this? Absolute nonsense – she couldn't speak to them any more than we could because the Proctors would not co-operate.

When describing the family around the boys, Jones lists *". . . Dad, John, age 53 & his wife of 11 yrs, Tessa, age 42, . . ."* and further on, *"Mom, Pamela Roche, has a significant other, Edward . . ."*

This starts to look like the most childish attempt to discredit me in whatever ways possible. Why can JP be shown as being married, and yet I am shown to have *"a significant other"*, when Edward and I had, in fact, been married since June 1994? This is so unacceptable. And yet, here we are, reading yet another missive by yet another of these amazing 'professionals'.

"His GMO says he was in a coma & almost died when at age 4 but she can't recall what the doctors said."

This is referring to the febrile seizure, obviously. But which professional wouldn't want to check out those details? How can that not be significant?

"Developmental history is only sketchily known since Mom was not an informant . . ."

So Dr Jones was happy, satisfied, confident, to proceed without a proper developmental history? He only had to pick up a telephone and ask the questions. But no – once again, I am kept out, ignored, overlooked, not important in the grand scheme. 'Mom' has been trying her damnedest throughout this sorry saga *to be an informant*, but she isn't allowed to have a voice.

The report is, in my opinion, an utter waste of time and money. It ends in the same fantasy world as it began: *"The passage of time in a safe & structured environment is clearly helpful."*

"Safe and structured"? In which madman's opinion is the Proctor household either safe or structured? The boys are isolated, and, by their own admission, have no friends, no sports or hobbies.

And finally, proving that Jones didn't even know why he was doing this, he pays homage to the erroneous Dr Gomez. *"His current care seems helpful, combining meds & therapy to deal w/ his [Joss'] issues."*

Would someone kindly explain to the good doctor that the reason he was asked to do this was because the court decided that perhaps Dr Gomez *wasn't* doing a very good job?

The report gave the diagnosis of Post Traumatic Stress Disorder. It didn't mention the other diagnoses, including childhood psychosis, Asperger Syndrome, not to mention Ryan's diagnosis, and not a word about the Order stating that Joss was to be removed from Dr Gomez' care and that Dr Jones was to be the new psychiatrist.

The report was issued to Dr Gomez and to the therapist, Deena Thomas. No copy was sent to Hoffmann. Why not?

I begin to run out of adjectives to describe this fiasco. It is little wonder that, when Edward finally succeeded in making contact with Dr Jones, his comment was a rather subdued "*I have been misled*". And, to add further insult to even further injury – I was supposed to pay half of Jones' fees!

So, another document full of the same lies and accusations – never proved – to cause me and Edward more damage, but not to help address the real problem here – the state of the boys and how to deal with that.

Jones had been fed the PTSD diagnosis and he hadn't even questioned it. He hadn't questioned anything – because he didn't know that's what he was supposed to be doing.

Why hadn't Hoffmann – as the children's lawyer – contacted Jones to brief him as to his input in this case?

Or, the bigger question, why was Hoffmann doing nothing at all to help the boys when his position was to protect their interests?

Chapter twenty-two

more of the worst

Daniella was now three years old. We were still numb, reeling from having lost our battle for custody just months earlier. We were in a state of shock and disbelief – that feeling you get when life suddenly thrusts you into something so unreal and terrifying, you are certain it's the worst nightmare you ever had, and any moment now you'll wake up and life will be good again.

But there was no waking up.

In July 2002, in an attempt to get away, to escape from the reality that was on the verge of destroying us, we took a holiday in France at my sister's place. Daniella had lost some weight and was particularly grumpy; when we had taken her to other children's parties she would cry and cling to me more than usual. I just put it down to toddler tantrums and didn't have any reason to take it more seriously. For the week in France she didn't have much of an appetite and we noticed some bruising around her ankles – this was probably from the tiled steps in the pool, we thought. Back home in England, more bruising appeared – some even on her back – and now she had tiny red spots all over her. A hasty visit to our GP put our minds at rest with the advice that this was no more than a post-viral reaction. Later the same week her condition was worse, and we noticed some bleeding inside her mouth. We dashed her to a different GP who had the good sense to refer us to Poole Hospital for blood tests. The results of these tests revealed that our precious little girl had leukaemia. Our new child, just three years old, had cancer.

I didn't sleep at all that night. I just sat in a chair, holding Daniella close to me, and I cried silently, hopelessly, until another day brought its light and its harsh reality to make me face what was happening to our lives, to our family.

Leukaemia is cancer of the blood or bone marrow and it is characterised by the abnormal increase in white blood cells. The bruising we had seen was caused by the lack of platelets in her blood which stop any bleeding.

The next day, we went to a larger hospital in Southampton where they had a special children's cancer ward: we spent six weeks there, sitting with Dani all day and sleeping in a little house that had been set up by a charity for use by parents of the childhood cancer victims. I'll never forget that place. Children and teenagers with no hair, their parents trying to smile through their heartache. Some of these children didn't leave this ward alive.

On our second day there, the consultant came to speak to us after Dani had had some tests. She had the type of leukaemia known as Acute Lymphoblastic Leukaemia, which is the common type of leukaemia found in children and which was well known to respond successfully to chemotherapy. Dani's case was different because her leukaemic cells had only half the number of chromosomes they should have, making it a particularly aggressive form of cancer. There had been just eight previous known cases of this rare condition, of which, sadly, only two had survived.

It was decided that the best form of treatment would be a bone marrow transplant – which meant finding someone who would be a match for Dani; apparently, only thirty per cent of patients ever found a match in those days. No match was found so there was no choice but to begin the chemotherapy. Due to the high risk of relapsing, the chemo was the most intensive regime possible. Because the chemo killed off the good cells as well as the bad ones, Dani went through periods of being neutropenic, meaning if she so much as caught a cold, she would have to spend more time in hospital having antibiotics. She was being given so many drugs, they ran a line straight to her heart.

Dani's chances of survival were quoted as twenty per cent. I was devastated. Terrified that she would relapse at any time, I felt that my entire family was being taken from me and it became something of an obsession. Losing the boys made this so much more difficult for me and I was constantly worrying, dreading what was around each corner.

It was as if I had become so familiar with the worst always happening, no matter what I did, there could be no other option but more of the worst.

We had two years of this, the first year in and out of hospitals a lot, but the second year was made slightly easier to manage because the chemo was administered in tablet form.

What happened to little Dani made me even more determined to have another child, especially since a new sibling would perhaps provide a match in case she did relapse.

This time, I fell pregnant quickly and little Hugo was born in June 2003 – a beautiful baby boy, a little brother for Dani. Of course, his arrival brought us great joy, but, unfortunately, he wasn't a match for Dani. Thankfully, she eventually went into remission and didn't need the chemo any longer. That never stopped me worrying, but her hair grew back and she became stronger and stronger as time passed.

This awful experience, on top of what had only just happened with Joss and Michael, stood to change my life completely. I became someone who valued the little things in life, I no longer concerned myself with trivia, and I learned to be extremely grateful for the blessings life had given me.

Chapter twenty-three

a glimmer of hope

A letter dated the thirtieth of July, 2002, was sent from the office of a Dr Steven C. Gabriel in San Diego – a letter which, I would imagine, raised a few eyebrows. It was simply addressed To Whom It May Concern . . .

> *"I have been asked to make myself available for a telephone interview regarding the evaluation (or lack thereof) and treatment of the Proctor children by Dr Gomez.*
>
> *I was hired as a medical consultant in the custody matter regarding these children and was shocked at the early initiation of potent drug therapy without adequate mental status evaluation of the subject child. The child was never evaluated while not under the influence of potent psychotropics. The family and patient appeared to have been seduced into a long term drug dispensing relationship with Dr Gomez that may have been motivated by money. There appears to have been no effective effort to understand the child's baseline psychiatric state. His approach seemed to encourage a relentless dependence on drugs, a marked deterioration in the child's function which may be related to the psychotropics and frequent office visits that did not bring the child into focus but do generate recurring office charges. These behaviours by the Doctor should be*

scrutinized as well as any similar practice patterns with other
children that may be discovered.
  Please contact me to arrange a phone interview in advance
so I can prepare for the discussion.
  Thank you,
  Steven C. Gabriel, M.D."

Dr Gabriel had been appointed by Ryan to come on board as
an independent consultant for the case. I paid his retainer, as
required, of two thousand, five hundred dollars. Dr Gabriel
never even got as far as seeing the boys and – surprise, surprise
– another unearned fee I had paid and I never saw anything
for my money.

Imagine my surprise, shock and amazement to read this
brief but incisive report by someone who has only just been
made aware of the case and yet sees so clearly the erroneous
and unacceptable medical practices by the staggeringly
inappropriate Dr Gomez.

I couldn't wait to see what happened next.

As you will no doubt imagine, July of that year and the months
that followed were not a good time for me to have to
concentrate on anything other than my little girl's dreadful
illness. As someone still needed to be the point of contact with
regard to what was (or wasn't) going on overseas, my brother
very kindly offered to help by writing to Hoffmann after
speaking to him towards the end of August. His letter said
that Dr Jones had not contacted me to discuss the situation
with me, nor to ask me for any medical records, nor to advise
me of the outcome of the consultation with Joss. In fact, the
only information we were getting was whatever Joss himself
told me during our telephone contact. This letter was faxed to
Hoffmann on the second of September, 2002.

"When we first spoke you mentioned that you would look into this and respond shortly. I then telephoned you again and you told me that you had not been able to speak to those who would be able to tell you the present position, but that you would do so by the end of last week, when you would provide me with an explanation that I could pass on to Pamela. I haven't heard from you since."

The letter ended with a request for Hoffman to telephone my brother and, to this end, provided both home and office telephone numbers.

I wrote a letter to Dr Jones on the tenth of September, following on from the telephone conversation we had four days earlier. Enclosed was a copy of Ryan's report to the State Board of Psychologist Examiners in Santa Fe, and a copy of Dr Gabriel's letter stating his *"opinion about the unethical conduct of Dr McKay and Dr Rowe, and psychiatrist Dr Gomez".* For good measure, I also enclosed a copy of the letter Hoffmann had sent to my lawyer and JP's lawyer on the thirteenth of March, drawing his attention specifically to the third paragraph: *"I recommend an updated psychiatric evaluation of Joss. As you may be aware, Joss has had several diagnoses by the psychologists and/or psychiatrists working with him or evaluating him. Dr Rowe stated that Joss has childhood psychosis, Dr Thomas believes Joss may have Asburger's* [Asperger] *Syndrome and Dr Gomez recently informed Ms Proctor that Joss continues to have post-traumatic stress disorder. Clearly, Joss needs to be reevaluated by a child psychiatrist in order to accurately diagnose his condition and to make sure Joss is taking the appropriate medication(s) and the correct amount of such medication(s). Dr Thomas has recommended William Jones, M.D., as the new psychiatrist . . ."*

Ryan's report to the State Board consisted of fourteen pages and it told precisely and informatively how the whole case began to career off-track because of mis-management by one professional, and how, from that point forward, each and every one of those involved in their respective professional capacity were led down the wrong road as a direct result of that initial blunder.

"Dr McKay compromised her professional and ethical integrity by providing a parent and his attorney, John Proctor and Michael Bolton Esq., with a letter to influence the court to give temporary custody of the Proctor children to Mr Proctor. Dr McKay prepared her letter based on one interview contact with Mr Proctor and his children. Attorney, Michael Bolton, contacted Dr McKay initiating the referral.

Dr McKay initially referred Mr Proctor to Child Protective Services (CPS), the appropriate place and personnel for allegations of abuse raised by Mr Proctor. Mr Proctor tells Dr McKay that CPS could not investigate his allegations. Next, Dr McKay contacts CPS to follow up on what Mr Proctor told her. CPS informs Dr McKay that the Proctor children are in the primary legal and physical custody of their mother and stepfather residing in England with UK citizenship. CPS informs Dr McKay that if Mr Proctor is concerned about allegations of abuse that Mr Proctor needs to report these concerns to the CPS authorities in England, and in the jurisdiction where the children are legally residing. England has mandatory child abuse reporting laws and mandated reporters, which is modelled in the same manner as in the United States. Based on my investigation I learned that England takes pride in their child social services delivery systems, especially their Child Protection Social Services.

Dr McKay fails to comply with the advice given by CPS,

and takes it upon herself to use her status as a psychologist to give Mr Proctor a letter recommending the court change custody. Dr McKay neglects to contact the custodial parents, the children's primary care medical doctor, or the school personnel where these children had been living for 9 years. Based on one interview, Dr McKay makes a recommendation without obtaining consent from the custodial parent, absent a court appointment, and absent critical information from the custodial family in the context of a custody dispute."

". . . In my opinion, John [Proctor] co-opted Dr McKay to opine that Joss and Michael were abused children and to recommend temporary custody to Mr Proctor. In my opinion, Dr McKay was blind sighted and did not detect John's agenda."

"In my opinion, Dr McKay's conclusions had a significant influence on a chain of service providers resulting in misinterpretations leading to misdiagnoses and improper treatment of the Proctor boys."

The next part of the report deals with the scientific principles that McKay's actions had violated.

Reading further to March 2000 when school staff and McKay had reported Joss as being severely paranoid, delusional and psychotic: *". . . Dr McKay recommended hospitalisation opining that Joss was gravely disabled . . . The Proctors did not follow up on the hospitalization recommendation . . . they presented their history to Dr Gomez. Given the paranoid and delusional symptoms exhibited by Joss and the alleged history of chronic and severe abuse, Dr Gomez concluded that the allegations of abuse were legitimate."*

The report details the failures of Dr Rowe, namely, that he

failed to produce the two psychological tests that JP was supposed to have taken; that he lied about having used McKay's records to assist in his recommendations and yet she said under oath that he never spoke to her nor did he review any of her records; Rowe should have taken into account the low score applied to Joss on the UK standardised national achievement test as being in some part related to having taken the test only days before flying to the States to live with JP, and he should have checked earlier test results which showed Joss' base line data as being 'average' range on national norms; and Rowe had told the court that Joss had shown some ambivalent feelings towards me, when in fact it was quite the reverse.

"The issue of ambivalence for Dr Rowe substantiated his clinical decision that alienation was not a factor in this case." Hoffmann, however, who had been present at the meeting referred to, informed Ryan that Rowe had been making this up because there was definitely no ambivalence.

On the subject of co-operation from other professionals (or the lack thereof), the report *says "Dr Rowe, on the other hand, did not follow through with furnishing me with missing documents in his file, nor did he return calls."*

"Dr Rowe exhibited a pattern of neglecting to return anyone's calls or responding to correspondence, including court orders. Mr Hoffmann informed me that Dr Rowe's conduct was like this for all of Dr Rowe's cases that Mr Hoffmann was aware of."

When pushed to produce the missing test for JP, Rowe, after promising to bring the papers to court and not doing so, suddenly said he remembered not receiving the results from National Computer Systems, Inc., blaming them for losing the tests.

Then the report covers Dr Gomez and his absolute refusal to return anyone's calls or correspondence, creating problems for the other professionals. *"Dr McKay, Dr Rowe and I made concerted efforts to confer with Dr Gomez who failed to return any of our calls, so none of the assessment or treatment service providers have been able to speak with Dr Gomez, who is prescribing the medication for Joss."*

Dr Gomez' efforts to avoid meeting Ryan were included, along with his conscious deception in having Ryan sent to an office which was vacated, and his denial of knowing who it was Ryan was enquiring about.

The report continues to highlight even more failings in the system, in that the latest court order was not being carried out. *"The court ordered that Dr Gomez' treatment of Joss Proctor stop immediately and for the Proctors, with the supervision of Mr Hoffmann, Esq., to find a competent pediatric psychiatrist to obtain a proper diagnosis and treatment protocol.*

I have reason to believe that Dr Gomez is not aware of the January court orders and that he continues to treat and prescribe a polypharmacy medication regimen for Joss. I have reason to believe that now after 6 months since the court made the initial orders that the new pediatric psychiatrist has not been obtained. The court further ordered that the new psychiatrist contact me about my report and contact Joss and Michael's mother and stepfather, including obtaining all the medical records from England. As of July 23, 2002, Mrs Roche informed me that the new psychiatrist had not come on board and that Joss was still seeing Dr Gomez."

The summary of this report explained: *"The court made a finding that all the allegations of abuse, especially the sexual abuse allegations against mother and stepfather were false. However, the court was confused as to why the Proctor children protested so strongly when they arrived in December 1999 about wanting to stay with their father and stepmother and hating their mother and stepfather. With respect to my report and testimony about parental alienation being the most probable hypothesis and explanation, the court made a finding that father, Mr Proctor, has alienated these children."*

Then there is an explanation of the court's confusion as to when alienation would have taken place, and whether this was the children's doing or the father's and stepmother's, and there was no decision on this particular query.

Then the report details a very important aspect. *"The court did not believe that it was in the realm of reality that 2 children could be so severely alienated in a matter of a couple of months to within a period of 3 weeks. The research on this issue is clear, that a thought reform program or emotional and psychological manipulation of a child by powerful adults can occur in a matter of hours to a couple of days. The issue of intervals of time for alienation to occur depends on 'context' and in many situations, the children's natural feelings of affection toward a parent are significant factors in the process of the child being emotionally manipulated."*

"The court was very distressed about how disturbed the Proctor children appeared in chambers, especially after hearing testimony about their disturbed behaviour. The judge stated that he had never seen anything like what he experienced when he met Joss and Michael in chambers. The judge said he was angry and blamed father for the condition the children were in."

This very thorough report ends with *"I have reason to believe that the courts orders and intention for the children to reunite with their mother have failed for the reasons outlined in my report.*

I appreciate the opportunity I had to evaluate this case. Please do not hesitate to contact me if you need more information or have questions.

Sincerely yours, Dr Ryan Brand Licensed Psychologist, August 1, 2002"

This report basically says it all, shows all of the mis-management, the lying, cheating, avoidance tactics – everything I had been trying to get everyone to see, to listen to, to comprehend. All set out neatly and professionally over fourteen pages.

And yet – to prove to me that I was never going to get anywhere in this battle for justice – no action was taken against McKay, Rowe or Gomez. They were never taken to task for any part of the catalogue of errors, oversights, breaches of ethics . . . nothing.

I used to believe in justice.

On the eleventh of September, Edward and I faxed Hoffmann to say that I had made contact with Dr Jones on the sixth of that month, and I was concerned that Hoffmann had not returned either my brother's calls, or my own.

> *"When my brother finally did establish contact with you, you claimed to be waiting for Dr Jones to return your calls.*
> *Dr Jones informed me that he had no knowledge of calls from yourself and is indeed mystified about why he has been misled about the purpose of his involvement in Joss' treatment and evaluation.*
>
> *I have now instructed my lawyer to inform Judge McDougall about recent events.*
>
> *I await your explanation with interest."*

Michael Keene was also arranging to meet with the judge to bring him up to speed with recent events. There was to be a hearing in November and I was to take part by telephone. It was only then that I received Dr Jones' report.

It's difficult to pinpoint any one specific major flaw in this whole episode, but I do feel strongly that the Jones part of this shows clearly what a complete sham the legal system is – bearing in mind this centres around the undeniably critical aspect of child protection. Court orders that are issued but never enforced, so they can be flouted with no repercussions whatsoever: perhaps the worst thing that would happen was a mild 'slap on the wrist', no more than that.

So much money is spent on lawyers, court officials, court reporters and all that goes with a court case. And the end result? The judge issues a court order, then . . . nothing. Nobody bothers to obey the court order, and nobody does anything about it.

In my case, the judge told the Proctors that they must stop alienating the children. Once they were back home, they were free to do whatever they wanted and there would be absolutely no comeback.

Here I was, a year after the judge had made the order, and I was spending even more money taking this *back* to court because none of what had been ordered had been followed through. I had learned from this bitter experience that court orders are not worth the paper on which they are typed.

Chapter twenty-four

back to court

November 2002 and another court hearing, only, this time, I wasn't flying halfway around the globe – my 'appearance' was to be by telephone.

Michael Keene opened the proceedings by explaining that my complaint was that Joss was still under the 'care' of Dr Gomez, when the order had stated that he should be removed from Gomez' supervision. He slipped in his comment that, when we tried to serve Gomez with the subpoena, he had literally run away from us! Also, we had only just received Dr Jones' report that morning, which was four months later, and it had only turned up then because I had insisted on seeing it. I was being kept completely out of the picture and it was only by paying yet more legal fees that I could have this aired again in court to try to get someone to do something about it. Michael added that I was unhappy that things were repeatedly pushed back, because no-one was monitoring or intervening.

The judge asked Michael *"What do you recommend I do so your client feels more involved?"* and Michael responded *"I would like Mr Hoffmann to be more involved in scheduling appointments to avoid more delays"*, meaning that, if the Proctors weren't left to their own devices all the time, they wouldn't be able to keep cancelling and postponing everything. The judge said he was granting this request.

Yes, I had lost the custody case, but I was not going to lie down and be quiet. I wanted to make sure my boys received whatever treatment they needed, make sure they were being looked after. All the court orders in the world couldn't stop me being their mother. These people thought that, if they kept me in the dark for long enough, I would eventually get fed up and go away. They could think again.

It was little wonder that the Jones report had been kept from me and my attorney. The contents were such a gross misrepresentation of any truth, and, that aside, the report was *not* what the court had asked for, because Jones had been so misled as to his role in the case. Hoffmann admitted there had been 'confusion' over Dr Jones' role and, when I took my turn to speak, I stressed that the doctor had been seriously misinformed: he was under the impression he was carrying out a straightforward, one-off review to ensure the medications being prescribed for Joss were correct. Of course they appeared correct, as per the assessment of Joss' condition carried out by Gomez, and so he confirmed this was so. What he was really supposed to be doing, was a full assessment of his own as to Joss' condition and needs.

Something else I hadn't been told about and only heard for the first time now, was that the Proctors were planning another move, this time from Abiquiu to Albuquerque. More spanners in the works.

Hoffmann explained that Joss was currently seeing Deena Thomas twice a week as part of the school's support for him, and she reported that Joss was showing signs of improvement. She had agreed to continue working with him after the planned move, but this would be in Santa Fe and would therefore probably not be free of charge any longer, and would need to be paid for.

In his usual stance of defending the Proctors to the hilt, Burke said they had no medical insurance to cover mental health work, and he quoted the cost of Joss' medication at six hundred dollars a month. He used this financial angle to justify why Joss was still seeing Gomez, who – because he was such a nice doctor – was supplying Joss' medication in the form of free drug samples given to the doctor by drug companies. So the Proctors didn't have to pay for those, nor were they paying for Deena Thomas, since her services were free as part of the school's support.

I thought it was appalling that Joss was being medicated with free samples of some very serious drugs, just because they couldn't afford to pay. I asked if this was possibly at odds with medical ethics? Then I argued that I would pay the psychiatrist and I would also pay the medication costs, such was my determination to get Joss away from Gomez.

It was agreed that this should be put back to Dr Jones to see if he could do the work, as originally planned. Of course, the subject of fees came up again. Burke – unstintingly defensive of the Proctors – reported that they had no money to pay any fees; all of this discussion seemed to be revolving around money and Burke was making it crystal clear that the Proctors wouldn't be footing any bills. I had no option but to offer to pay for all of Joss' medications and also for Dr Jones' fees, if he would take on the work. Anything to get Joss away from Gomez and, as I added, *"It's so urgent to get Joss the right treatment . . . someone needs to get to the bottom of what is wrong with Joss."*

The judge decided that, if I was to pay for the psychiatrist and the medication, then the Proctors should pay for Carol Kerr – at least the outstanding amount of six hundred dollars. He also suggested that the work for both boys just might come under the Medicare service, and, if so, *"Maybe we can transfer from Gomez to another psychiatrist."* Burke said JP would look into this possibility. The judge made the suggestion that Dr

Jones could review the medications periodically and then it would be perfectly OK for Gomez to prescribe.

Then Hoffmann was discussed. Amazingly, he admitted to everyone present that he had not taken any of my calls, nor returned them, and had not replied to any of my correspondence. The judge spoke up for him, saying he had known Hoffmann for years and that he was extremely trustworthy, which was why he had been assigned to this case.

Hoffmann may have been trustworthy in his dealings with others, but he certainly wasn't when dealing with me. The judge asked if he had an e-mail address to give me, to make communicating with him somewhat easier than the faxes we were having to send each time. Hoffmann said he didn't have e-mail. Really? An attorney with no e-mail in 2002? I think not. But he knew that faxing was much more difficult for me and he was, once again, trying to push me away.

I made the point that I wanted to travel back to the US for a supervised visit, at which Hoffmann tried to put me off the idea. He told the judge how awful the meeting with the boys had been in January, and reminded everyone that the boys had said they didn't want to see me or have any contact with me. He described the meeting as *"Nothing short of heartbreaking for Ms Roche. I would love these boys to have even a glimmer of a relationship with their mother."*

Yes, I agreed it wouldn't be easy, but that wasn't the point. The court order had stated that I was to have supervised visits at first, then unsupervised visits when that was feasible – and that JP should pay the expenses of such visits. I reminded them that Rowe had said in court, and in his report, that the children should be reintegrated with me as soon as possible, and that they were looking forward to this taking place.

This had been Rowe's famous argument that, because the boys had 'shown ambivalence' towards me, this couldn't be a PAS case. I knew this was complete rubbish and I was prepared to prove it in the only way I could. A lot of parents, I suppose, wouldn't want to put themselves through such a painful experience, but I was determined to show these people that I wouldn't just go away.

Following that court hearing, I contacted Dr Jones to ask him if he would take on the work with Joss as requested by the court. He was not at all keen to do this, due to the case being subject to legal proceedings. Plus, I suppose, he had already had a taste of dealing with the Proctors and seeing how they twisted the truth of the situation, even though they were supposed to be carrying out the instructions of a court order. No professional would want to put themselves in such an obviously tricky situation.

Although I have to appreciate his position, I would have thought Dr Jones could at least have contacted Hoffmann to discuss the matter with him as the children's guardian, as another professional – even if he didn't want to undertake the actual work. I also find it quite alarming that he had taken every word the Proctors fed to him as fact, especially bearing in mind that this information was given to him by the eighty-two-year-old granny.

I explained to Dr Jones about the court order, telling him he hadn't been given clear guidelines as to the issues he was supposed to be dealing with. I made it clear to him that I had seen his appointment as a very positive move and had been looking forward to seeing the results of his input. I told him, if he was to withdraw from the case, I really couldn't see any realistic prospect of being able to address my concerns about Joss' treatment. I really did try to persuade him.

All to no avail, and my efforts got me nowhere. Another suitable psychiatrist had to be found, which would take more time. More time meant more delays – delays Joss couldn't afford.

I called Ryan and asked him for advice. He contacted his

sponsor in New Mexico, Christopher Allander, and asked if he could recommend anyone. Dr Richards' name was put forward and it was agreed that Joss should see her. For one more time, I was being given new hope. I spoke to Dr Richards on the phone to give her a brief history of the case along with Joss' current psychiatric condition; I told her that two very conflicting reports had been written and that Joss had had many differing diagnoses. I stressed that what Joss needed was for someone to really get to the bottom of what was wrong with him.

Dr Richards confirmed that she was a practitioner in child and adolescent general psychiatry, but she said she tried to avoid evaluations that required formal typed reports to be produced, as she didn't have a secretary. I have to say, I heard faint alarm bells on hearing this, but we went on to discuss fees and I paid her an up-front retainer of fifteen hundred dollars to get her to begin working with Joss. I convinced myself that Dr Richards would have to produce a report of some kind, once she had studied the history of the case, Joss' medical history and the various professionals' reports. I was just so desperate to get things moving, to get Joss away from this awful abusive situation.

Eventually, Joss did go to see her – but only once. Why? Because the Proctors announced they were moving home *again* – this time out of State, to Austin in Texas. Yet another escape for them, yet more wasted money for me, as I never received any refund of the retainer I paid Dr Richards. The Proctors hadn't moved to Albuquerque, as they had said they were intending to do in November, but had remained in Abiquiu.

What on earth could I do now? I couldn't prevent them from moving home if that's what they wanted to do, but this new move would make it very difficult for the court orders to be enforced, as they would be living many miles away from where the judge was based. This was the Proctors making efforts to break completely away from the whole situation, taking themselves off the radar. Hoffmann would have been relieved at this, knowing how difficult it had already been for me to chase things up – he probably thought this latest manoeuvre would finally get rid of me.

This put me into a state of panic. I got Michael Keene to call the judge to update him on these most recent – and very important – developments. The judge said the Proctors would have to pay the same amount of retainer as I had paid Dr Richards, to another psychiatrist, this time in Austin. Dr Richards gave us three names of psychiatrists who she knew and was happy to recommend, and the Proctors were to appoint one of these.

Of course, when they did move to Austin in August 2003, that didn't happen because Hoffmann gave them permission to find their own psychiatrist.

Chapter twenty-five

another door closes

In May 2003, I received a letter from the New Mexico Board of Medical Examiners in Santa Fe which was their reply to the official complaint Ryan had submitted against Dr McKay, Dr Rowe and Dr Gomez. Ryan's report to them had consisted of fourteen pages of detailed, concise, professionally written content. The reply letter consisted of three paragraphs:

"Dear Mrs Roche,
The New Mexico Board of Medical Examiners has concluded its investigation of your complaint against Rene Gomez, M.D.
After careful review of your complaint they found no violation of the Medical Practice Act. Accordingly, no action will be taken against the medical license of Dr Gomez and **the complaint has been closed***.*
Thank you for sharing your concerns with the New Mexico Board of Medical Examiners. The information you provided has been entered into an informational database that is used to determine if there is a pattern of problems with individual physicians. Although the complaint is being closed, the information will be available for use in the future, if needed.
Sincerely,
Complaint Committee Chair"

How could they ignore such a report? How could they ignore Gabriel's comment that all of Gomez' case load should be examined for similar questionable practices?

The fact that those four words were displayed in bold type said everything to me. Go away, shut up! Leave this alone, get on with your own life, there's nothing here for you . . . and, once more, I felt that perhaps I *had* lost my mind completely and I was now living in total and utter madness.

Chapter twenty-six

another dead end

The court appointed therapist, Carol Kerr, had occasion to visit London at one point and thought it would be a good opportunity for her to meet us to discuss the way forward. She had been recruited to work with Michael and also to try to reintegrate us all as a family.

She was staying at an exclusive club in Mayfair and she suggested we meet at a rather salubrious place where Edward had to wear a tie to get in – not our usual kind of haunt.

We arrived, laden with our paperwork, reports, letters, photographs and so on. I don't think Ms Kerr was expecting anything like this: she had obviously been told we were abusers, which, in her mind, was confirmed by the fact that the judge had kept the boys in the US. She had the onerous task of trying to help re-form some kind of family relationship between the children and the people she believed had been abusing them for years on end.

We told her right off that this was a complete lie, and that she really must read Ryan's report. It's so difficult, when you meet someone for the first time and you want – need – to tell them so much, but it would take years to explain everything in the detail you want this person to understand, and this is made worse by knowing this person is giving you a limited amount of their time. We tried to get her to see that, no matter what the judge had said, no matter what court orders had been issued, we were not going to lie down and take this. We were not going to be seen as abusers when we were anything but, and we were not going to accept that I had to lose my children because of a catalogue of lies, deceit and poison.

We explained to her that reintegration would be impossible unless the boys were removed from the Proctor household, because this was a case of PAS. When we asked how familiar she was with PAS cases, she was very vague in her response and obviously didn't have much, if any, knowledge of the subject.

There was no way we were going to change our stance on this and it quickly became evident that this meeting was a waste of time.

Disappointed, we packed up our papers and returned home. Same old, same old. But we kept hoping against hope that, the more people who got involved, the more chance there was that someone would eventually 'get it'.

Chapter twenty-seven

holding on to hope

Dr Richards had seen Joss in April 2003, and the Proctors moved to Austin, Texas, in the August of that year. Instead of them appointing one of the three recommended psychiatrists put forward by Dr Richards, once again, the Proctors go their own way and completely ignore what the court had ordered. Hoffmann gave them permission to source a new psychiatrist of their own choosing.

As I had guessed, several months went by and I was kept totally out of the loop – no updates, no news – nothing. It was all so predictable.

Of course, I tried to keep myself in the picture: I sent numerous letters to Hoffmann, all of which he ignored, including one dated the seventeenth of November, 2003, in which I demanded to know which psychiatrist was working with Joss, also asking why none of the three recommended by Dr Richards had been appointed. I said *"Contrary to Judge McDougall's wishes there has been no reintegration with my sons. I have seen them a total of half-an-hour in 4 years which was in your office in your presence. I have been unable to come out between June 2002 – July 2003 due to my daughter's ongoing intensive chemotherapy. I have, however, been waiting to come out since then but have been unable to because there is nobody to meet. Who is going to supervise this visit? Months pass and nothing happens. This is not good enough.*" I ended the letter by asking to hear some news within the following week and telling Hoffmann that I wanted "*to make it very clear to everybody that I want to visit before Christmas.*"

I was asking for no more than the court had ordered, and yet, once again, no response whatsoever, no visit, and no contact with my sons.

Eventually, realising I was not going to get anywhere with this, I asked Michael Keene to write to him instead.

Eight months from the time when the Proctors should have appointed the new psychiatrist, I was finally given the name of Robert Dale, the therapist who had been working with the boys since January 2004. This was now April.

I'll never forget the e-mail from Michael Keene coming through, telling me Robert Dale was anxious to talk to me and hear my side of the story: he said he thought it was actually the Proctors who were contributing to the problems the boys were experiencing. I could scarcely believe it – was there finally someone involved who was not going to swallow whatever the Proctors' latest work of fiction happened to be, someone who would see what was really going on? With all of the many crippling disappointments behind me so far, could I even dare to build up some hope this time? The answer is clear – where your children are concerned, there has to be hope. Always.

I was desperate to fly out and meet this man. I couldn't help feeling excited – just those few words on the e-mail had me walking around in a daze for the rest of the day. That brief message was so encouraging, as much as I had learned from bitter experience not to believe anything positive was happening, I really couldn't avoid seeing this as a real breakthrough. At last, someone was questioning the situation.

My brain went into overdrive and I kept flashing forward in time, even to the point where the boys would be returned to the UK, to their proper home, to me. My emotions raced around in uncontrollable circles, speeding into and out of the many different possibilities until I was light-headed – but exhilarated for the first time in ages.

Edward and I flew out to Austin in May, and we found a place to stay quite close to Robert's therapy centre. He worked in a government funded family centre called the Travis County Mental Retardation Center, which had been set up to help those who had no medical insurance – a bit like a lower-level NHS.

Arriving at the office, our initial impression was the stark contrast of this place to the flashy, plush, expensively furnished suites belonging to those mental health workers and lawyers who we had visited previously. This was a place where dedicated people came to help those in need of their support. This was a place where seriously abused children were brought for therapy and medication and that is what Robert dealt with on a daily basis.

Robert, firstly, asked about something that had been confusing him since he had first met the Proctors. How come they lived in an expensive gated community, drove luxury cars, and yet, sent their children to this place for treatment? The Proctors had asked Robert to authorise another application for funding for the work he was doing, and he simply couldn't understand why – it didn't make sense.

Edward and I took an instant liking to Robert, from the moment we met. In his mid-thirties, and dressed casually in jeans and an open-neck shirt, he gave the impression of someone who really cared, someone doing a job because it *needed* to be done, not for the money or the glory. He showed us into his office and I started to blurt out everything about the boys, the court case, the history, the PAS – there was so much to tell and it was vital that he know and understand all of it. We gave him a load of paperwork to read and some information on PAS. He told us – and he told Hoffmann as well – that he didn't think the boys had been abused because *abused children do not behave like this.*

Eureka! At last – someone who has the knowledge and experience to see the reality of the boys' behaviour. This felt like seeing sunlight for the first time after years of cold, dark night.

Robert was very puzzled as to why there had been no CPS investigation of the case and so I explained that it was outside the jurisdiction of the American CPS and so should have been reported to the Child Protection Service in the UK, but the only person who had carried out any investigation in the UK was Ryan. I told Robert about the behaviour of the other professionals and how they had been reported to the State Board, but that nothing had come of the complaints.

We met the psychiatrist whose role was purely to administer Joss' medication. Along with therapy sessions with Robert, this had been the treatment regime for the past three months. Then I learned something that came as a shock. It appeared that it wasn't only Joss who was suffering with mental health problems, but Michael was being treated for depression, he was experiencing insomnia and was frequently wetting the bed. He had been getting into trouble at school so much that he was receiving home education (which I later found out went on for two years).

Robert described the Proctor household as chaotic, unstable and confusing. He said JP was mainly absent and, when he did appear, he would take centre stage and prattle on about his business deals, causing more chaos. Tess was unable to cope, Robert told us, which had led to her becoming mentally unstable. The picture unfolding before us was hideous, but no worse than I had imagined. He said Joss, in particular, needed to be in a family environment where there was love and stability in abundance. Robert was very concerned that living in such an unstable, chaotic home, with no apparent love or affection being shown, might lead to the boys harming either themselves or someone else. Robert explained that professionals involved in such cases needed to ensure safeguarding by enforcing the issue that the Proctors seek counselling, in case of any possible incident.

The elation of hearing all of the positive aspects of what Robert was saying was soon crushed by the supervised visit with the boys that followed. The hour passed exactly as I'd anticipated – after all, I'd been studying PAS so much that I knew basically what to expect.

The boys, of course, didn't want to see me. There was no hug or any physical contact, and they didn't even look directly at me. The whole time they kept checking their watches and saying things like *"Is that enough now? Can we go now?"*, and so on. What I really couldn't get my head around was that they were both smoking like chimneys! My two boys, puffing on cigarettes like two little old men – I found that very disturbing and a matter for concern. I know they were now four years older than last time I saw them – fourteen and fifteen – but to smoke openly, in front of adults? It was unsettling and shocking.

I was desperate to make the most of this precious hour, but how could I do that when the boys were being so openly antagonistic? I struggled for conversation . . . I asked what sort of music they liked, what were their bedrooms like at home, did they have any posters on the walls . . . I tried my hardest and Robert was brilliant – he made them sit through the whole hour, even though they made it clear they wanted to escape. It was such a difficult situation but Robert wouldn't give in. He knew the value of these visits, both for them and for me. I was so grateful for his support, and, after all, it was what the court had ordered.

A couple of days later, we had a second supervised visit,

equally horrendous. Robert made them stay for the full hour session again, despite their behaviour. They were furious that I was there, and they asked me where I was staying, who with, and so on. I think perhaps a lot of people would have burst into tears and fled from that room, but I had learned to develop a pretty thick skin since all of this began, and no way was I going to give the Proctors the satisfaction of knowing I couldn't handle this.

For a lot of the time, all I did was sit and look at the boys. Having not seen them for four years, they had changed quite a lot. These were the two little people I had seen almost every day for eleven years, and I just wanted to look at them so that I could hold their faces in my mind until I could see them again, and I couldn't know when that would be. For the past four years, all I could do was imagine how they would look, so I had to make the best of this short time. It was all so difficult, so hard for me, with them sitting there, not wanting to know me. Very painful.

While we were winding things up with Robert at the end of our stay, I asked him if he could help me get the boys away from the Proctors. My heart sank as he explained that his role as therapist meant he couldn't be involved in any legal proceedings – his job was to support the children and the family around the children.

But that wasn't the worst blow, after I had built up my hopes again. Robert was leaving to get married at the end of June. I was dreadfully disappointed that he was leaving, but he said he would, of course, introduce us to his successor when the new therapist took over.

On the twenty-fifth of May I wrote a letter to Hoffmann, the content of which was somewhat fuelled by the fact that I had received an invoice from him a few days before, asking for a payment of one thousand, two hundred and fifteen dollars and sixty-nine cents. I felt it was time to make a bit of a stand against this man who was supposed to be the boys' legal Guardian – a position carrying certain responsibilities which he was failing to uphold – but who was causing me all sorts of problems by basically refusing to have any contact with me or to keep me up to date.

I told him in this letter that I had not sent a payment for the invoice and listed the reasons why.

"As GAL it is your duty to facilitate communications, arrange appointments, ensure Court Orders are followed through and allow free flow of information between therapists and all parties, yet you have done the opposite at every turn."

"You failed to return all my phone calls and ignored all my correspondence in the year 2002."

"In January 2002 it was ordered that Joss should have an 'updated psychiatric evaluation' that should proceed 'as expeditiously as possible'. You allowed the Proctors to prevaricate until July 25th 2002 . . ."

"Dr Jones was misled by her [the grandmother] *that this was a one-off consultation to check levels of medication prescribed by Dr Gomez and I was written off as a 'non-informant'".*

"My brother tried to contact you many times whilst I was in hospital with my daughter about this matter and you failed to return his calls as well."

"You gave the Proctors free rein to inform psychiatrists/ therapists what was required by them always excluding myself."

"Judge McDougall stated that Joss had to be removed from Dr Gomez' care."

"I had to re-engage my attorney at further cost to myself because of these difficulties caused by you."

"The Proctors were in Austin for 8 months before the name of a psychiatrist/ therapist was revealed."

I referred to the current situation in Austin, mentioning that Robert Dale was baffled as to why there had been no CPS investigation after such allegations had been made.

"Although all the allegations were thrown out of Court . . . The Proctors are still presenting these allegations to therapists/ psychiatrists as true."

My list of complaints against Hoffmann poured on to the paper. I was so angry with this man, who was regarded as a professional Guardian of vulnerable children, but was doing such an appalling job. I ended by reiterating Robert's advice that the Proctors should seek counselling for themselves as a safeguarding measure in case either of the boys should attempt to harm themselves or anyone else, due to the instability and chaos that surrounded them in the Proctors' home.

And one final dig at Hoffmann – *"On past performance I have little faith that this will be followed through. You as GAL are the lynch pin in their legal status and as their mother I hold you morally responsible to follow it through."*

As far as payment of his invoice was concerned, I pointed out that JP owed me, as ordered by the court, expenses from the visit I had just had, which amounted to one thousand, one hundred and ninety-two dollars and seven cents. I enclosed receipts to cover this amount. I then told Hoffmann he had my permission to claim this money owed to me from JP and that he could keep it as payment of his invoice to me.

My final paragraph told of my intention to travel out for another supervised/ visit at the beginning of July to meet John Rendell, who was taking over from Robert Dale.

I copied the letter to Michael Keene.

Chapter twenty-eight

just for the hell of it

It was July 2004 when I decided to take JP to court for the hundred and twenty-five thousand dollars of child support arrears. Not – you understand – that I expected, for one second, that I would ever see one penny of this debt, I just wanted to cause him some aggravation for a while, be a thorn in his side. After all, he'd seemingly got away with so very much over the past five years and nobody had given him any grief, it was time to redress the balance, I thought.

This debt had been officially recognised by the court at the end of the trial, so why should I let JP get away with this and not even have to offer any explanation, let alone any payment? He also still owed the eighty thousand dollars which, although included in the legal papers we signed when we divorced, was treated as a totally separate issue from the child support.

There were no less than four separate hearings arranged and scheduled over the following nine months, and all of these were allowed to be postponed. By JP, of course. This postponement is referred to as a continued hearing. One of the marvellously creative excuses given by JP for the continuation – this time the hearing had been set for the ninth of November, 2004 – was, and I quote, *"Petitioner seeks to continue the November 9th 2004 hearing because his employer requires him to travel to*

Hong Kong the first week in November 2004. If Petitioner does not travel to Hong Kong, he faces demotion, or at worst, termination from his employment. More importantly, the travel is connected to a project that, if successful, will enable him to increase his income substantially, thus enabling him to make a meaningful settlement offer to resolve the issues herein."

I find it inconceivable that JP could be allowed to do this four times in succession without question, but he was. Yet again, he refused to toe the line with the court, and they just sat back and let him.

Chapter twenty-nine

a helping hand

Having had Robert Dale come along as my light at the end of a very long and very dark tunnel, I was despondent when he left. As much as I wished him every happiness in his new life, I couldn't help feeling a real sense of loss. But, trying to be positive, I assumed that whoever took over his post would read his report and case file, and would pick the case up from that point.

In the summer of 2004, I had an e-mail from Pamela Hoch at the Rachel Foundation, because I was on their mailing list. They were relocating to Texas – specifically, to Hill County just outside Austin, a tiny place called Harper. It struck me as rather coincidental that they were going to be situated really close to where my boys lived.

I got in touch with Pamela to tell her I was due to travel to Austin to meet John Rendell, who I had been informed was the replacement for Robert Dale, and I asked if I could possibly stay at the Foundation. She was delighted at this and said of course I could stay, which was a great relief for me to know I had some support out there.

I arranged my trip for October, and Pamela collected me from San Antonio airport. She drove us to Rachel House in Harper – a small home in a fairly isolated area, where I met her husband, Bob. It was so good to meet these two people, and I liked them both immensely, The house felt friendly and welcoming, and I instantly knew they both had an incredible knowledge and understanding of PAS, of alienation, of everything surrounding this dreadful form of abuse. I knew I was among friends and – amazingly – I was able to relax there. It reminded me of when Edward and I had stayed in that little centre while Dani was so desperately ill: all of the parents, even though they'd never met before, shared something so terrible, there was an air of real understanding, of genuine empathy and unspoken friendship.

I came to know Pamela and Bob quite well in the time I stayed with them before I met with John Rendell, and I listened to each of their stories. Hers was one of the first publicised cases of PAS when her divorce case in Quebec became one of the first recognised as a case of PAS, and that was in 1991. The case drew a lot of press attention at the time. Pamela managed to regain custody of two of her four children; the other two, unfortunately, remained hostile and alienated towards her. Pamela has since been asked to work full-time for the PAS Foundation in Washington, DC.

One thing they explained, which was most interesting to me, was that, in order for JP to obtain a *Temporary Custody Order*, the judge would have wanted to see evidence that he had paid the last four months child support. The only time in the whole ten years when he actually made payments to me was this particular period, just before he abducted the boys. At the time, I thought he must have finally got his business off the ground and that things were beginning to look up. Little did I know, he had an ulterior motive and it was all just another part of his plan.

I learned a lot from spending time with Pamela and Bob, and they kindly let me take advantage of their extensive library of books on PAS, on subjects such as psychopaths, and some books about cults – which have a lot in common with PAS. People who become trapped in a cult and are later rescued are treated in a very similar way to the methods used with PAS children. The only way to break the 'hold' is to remove the person from the environment in which they are trapped – the difference being, that with PAS cases, we are talking about children, not adults.

There was one book that caught my eye, entitled *Without Conscience*[5] written by Robert Hare, PhD, which I also read. As I turned each page, I began to realise the truth of the saying 'knowledge is power', because, the more I learned, the more I realised the deeper truth of what was going on, the more clearly I could see the whole dreadful picture.

This book is a *"fascinating, if terrifying, look at psychopaths . . . a chilling, eye-opening report"* (Kirkus Reviews) and the author has conducted influential research on psychopathy for over twenty-five years; he was, at the time of publication, Professor Emeritus of Psychology at the University of British Columbia, Canada and he developed one of the world's most widely used tools for assessing psychopathy. He wrote over one hundred professional articles and several books.

The book begins, quite wisely, with a cautionary note to the reader, not to assume that someone is a psychopath simply because they appear to fit the list of traits described in the book as those of a psychopath – a bit like you can hear a list of physical symptoms of some dreadful illness and quite easily believe you have it! However, while reading, I experienced many instances of shock recall, as my mind jumped back to something that had happened, something JP had done or said, and it was most disturbing to find so many examples in those pages that equated absolutely to this man, the father of my two boys. Almost everything described by the author

5 *Without Conscience, Robert D. Hare, PhD, published by The Guildford Press, New York and London 1999.*

– behavioural aspects, attitudes and characteristics – all reflected everything I knew about JP.

"*. . . the indifference to being identified as a liar is truly extraordinary.*"

Under the chapter heading 'Lack of Response', Hare says "*obligation and commitment mean nothing to psychopaths . . . truly horrendous credit histories, for example, reveal the lightly taken debt, the shrugged-off loan, the empty pledge to contribute to a child's support . . . they do not honour formal or implied commitments to people, organisations or principles.*"

At one point, sitting there on my own in that comfortable, welcoming place, reading all of these very interesting books, I looked up and glanced out of the window. What was I doing here, in the middle of Texas, learning about cults and psychopaths? The thought was so absurd, it made me smile for a moment, but I knew I was in the right place. Pamela and Bob were so good to me, but their charity was dreadfully underfunded and they were struggling financially. It was incredibly sad that these people had devoted their lives to helping the victims and children of PAS, in a world where PAS was as yet almost unrecognised. But they had sacrificed everything because they believed in the cause; PAS was their whole life, not just a hobby or even a career – they ate, slept, breathed and lived for the charity.

Pamela took me to the Mental Health and Retardation Center to meet John Rendell and to have my visit with the boys. They didn't want to see me, of course, but I knew that anyway, and this was yet another harrowing supervised visit; but I wasn't going to forego the chance to see Michael and Joss, however bad it was. Pamela waited for me in her car in the car park, and I could see the Proctors in their pick-up truck.

In John Rendell's office, I was trying to compose myself after the visit. I tried to explain to him what was happening here, that it was not a case of abuse on our part, but how it was the Proctors who had damaged the boys' young minds. I could see, as I spoke to him, that he had already formed his own opinion – even the literature I handed him was obviously of no interest. He simply didn't 'get it', even though he must have read Robert's case notes and report.

I remember the tears were streaming down my face as I tried desperately to explain to him what had happened. I had waited for months to see this man, and I had remained hopeful, given what Robert had told me and had put in his notes. John Rendell was my last hope and he just wasn't going to help me. I knew from all of my previous experiences that there were two very separate worlds concerning PAS. There were those who had opened their minds to the existence of something that was very real but simply had not been recognised until recently, and there were those who seemed to want to remain oblivious to any new information or knowledge – people who were almost afraid to step outside of their own familiar circle, people who needed to stick with the 'old thinking' and didn't dare take a look into any new ideas. John Rendell was obviously of the latter world.

He told me that Joss had been diagnosed with 'major depression with psychotic features' – not PTSD which the Proctors had been presenting to everyone to support their abuse accusations. This broke my heart, to know that my son was living in this highly dysfunctional family and was so seriously ill, desperately needing the proper care and not getting it. My hands were constantly being tied. I was devastated.

I left his office and walked to Pamela's car. As soon as I was in the passenger seat, Pamela told me what had been happening while I was in the office. The Proctors had driven their truck right up to her car bonnet, as if they were going to ram her vehicle, revving their engine while they glowered at her through the windscreen. A pathetic attempt to intimidate her, to scare off anyone who dared to be 'on my side'. They were obviously annoyed that I was there, and they had no idea who Pamela was, where I was staying, or even how I was managing to do all of this. It must have really bothered them.

When the time came for me to leave Rachel House, I was so moved at how completely selfless Pamela and Bob were, how totally giving of themselves to the work they were doing. I felt somehow different in myself after my time with them, and I knew I, too, had to do something for this cause. The feeling of determination to do this was almost overwhelming – the more I had learned about the victims of PAS, the more my anger grew. Anger at JP, anger at his parents, anger at the courts, the supposed professionals, the system, the law, the Hague Convention – all of it! I just knew I had to somehow use this energy to play my own part in exposing the dirty little secret that was PAS, and this driving force is what has led me to write this book today.

Chapter thirty

more about money

And then – the surprise twist. In February, 2005 we received from JP's lawyers masses of paperwork called *Requests for Admissions*, which were attempts to delve into our financial situation. They were trying to turn the tables on us and were actually demanding child support payments from us for the time when JP had had the boys with him. And, not just that. They were asking for money to cover future costs as well. The seventy-four page document included lots of questions we were supposed to answer, but some of these were so ridiculous as to be almost laughable. Can you believe, *"how much do you spend on petrol, babysitters, books, videos, nails, haircuts, pet expenses, gifts, cards"* – and even postage stamps! That's just a tiny snapshot of the almost endless reams of absurd questions.

Edward and I were so angered, affronted and insulted by this crass stupidity that we wrote a statement declaring our reasons for not supplying the details as requested. It began *"We refuse to provide Mr Burke with any of the documents he has requested. The situation is absurd and here are the reasons why."*

Once again, we listed facts such as, I had received no financial support from JP since the divorce in 1990; Edward had supported the boys since July 1991 even though they were not his own children; there was no evidence whatsoever of any abuse; because JP had failed to appoint a new psychologist, as ordered by the court, I had been forced to go back to court, incurring me in even more expense . . . and so on. I had said these same things now so many times, I could reel them off on demand.

We mentioned the glaring query we had had for so long about the Proctors' situation: *". . . Does that imply that JP has no medical insurance for his children? How irresponsible is that? Everybody has medical insurance in America. It's very strange that he can afford to live in a large house on a golf course in a gated community in Austin and drive new cars yet not have medical insurance . . . The children are currently being treated for their psychiatric disorders by a therapist and psychiatrist at a government funded medical center in Austin. It is my understanding that these places cater for the very poor."*

We included the failure of Hoffmann to ensure the Proctors sought counselling, as advised by Robert Dale, in case the boys attempted to harm anyone. We said Rowe's report had been proved to be a complete misrepresentation of the truth, that Judge McDougall's order that the boys should be reintegrated with me had not been carried out, as I had seen the children for a total of four hours over the previous five years.

We mentioned that JP had not reimbursed me for the costs of my visits, which was court ordered; we stated that we were offering to pay for the private psychiatric assessment which Robert Dale had recommended, and we ended with *"We have paid approximately $100,000 in legal/psychologist fees in the last 5 years not to mention the numerous trips and all the expenses that has entailed. For Mr Burke to dare to suggest delving into our finances at this stage has left us feeling outraged."*

Even though the court had recognised the large amount of money JP owed me, he had managed to file a *Counter Petition for Child Support* immediately after the 2002 court hearing. This stated that I should pay him child support, going back to December 1999 and remaining in force until the boys reached the age of eighteen. It also asked that I pay all expenses relating to any visits I might make in future, that I pay half of all therapy and related costs, half of Hoffmann's fees . . .

So, overlooking the fact that I (and later, Edward) had paid for everything relating to the boys for all of the time they were with me, including paying their air fares to visit their father, overlooking the fact that the sum of money he had legally committed to pay towards a house in England for us had never been paid, overlooking the fact that JP had fabricated all of those foul accusations against me and Edward, which have never been proven because they never took place, overlooking the fact that this man had caused his two young children to be separated from their own mother for over two years, and in the worst possible circumstances, overlooking the fact that he had poisoned the boys against me when I had done nothing wrong, overlooking the fact that I was many thousands of dollars out of pocket . . . overlooking *all* of this, he was now demanding that *I pay him*, not only child support, but also *"a pro-rata contribution from the Respondent for reimbursement for the therapy and counselling of the parties' minor children"*. Therapy and counselling that he had created the need for and which were not being managed or administered correctly.

In April 2005, following the four non-existent continued hearings, the Sandoval County Court issued a *Stipulated Order Settling Financial Matters*: the basic decision in this Order was that we were seen to be in a complete 'contra' situation, and that, *"As of April 4, 2005, Petitioner (Father) has fully satisfied all child support obligations to Respondent (Mother) arising out (of) the prior Texas orders on the same issues of on-going child support and child support arrears.*

As of April 4, 2005, Respondent (Mother) has fully satisfied all past child support obligations owed to Petitioner (Father), including reimbursement of out of pocket medical costs."

And, the amazing part, *"In light of the difficulty of establishing either parents' income, and in support of all of the other compromises and agreements contained within this Stipulated Order, Mother shall not pay Father any on-going child support for the remainder of the childrens' minority".*

I was a housewife and mother, on no earnings whatsoever. What 'difficulty' did they have in working that out? He was CEO (or, according to his testimony, he thought that was what they called him!) of a company. What was there to establish? He earned money and I did not. But, even on this subject, I was in a no-win situation with these people, and they showed me in the records as being in receipt of twelve dollars an hour – a random figure they had simply plucked out of the air!

The Order also said I had to pay all costs relating to any visits I had with the boys, but, as I had always done so, this was no big deal for me. I was also ordered to pay half of Hoffmann's fees, even though he was not doing his job at all properly, and, no matter how many times I complained about him, it never got me anywhere.

Just like everything I had tried to do over the past five and a half years.

Chapter thirty-one

let down again

When I arrived back home after my meeting with John Rendell, I thought about the latest diagnosis Joss had been given – 'major depression with psychotic features' – and I wondered if I could try to get a second opinion. Maybe find someone with experience of PAS to provide this? To my amazement, because John Rendell considered this a reasonable idea, and because, of course, I was footing the bill, Hoffmann actually allowed me to decide who to appoint. There was a psychologist who was associated with the Rachel Foundation called Jack Farrow, who had also worked previously with Ryan, so he was familiar with this type of case and seemed the ideal candidate.

In March 2005, I contacted John Rendell, who informed me that he hadn't been working with the Proctor family for quite some time; I'm fairly certain that he must have left the treatment centre shortly after I had seen him in October 2004. I asked who Joss' psychiatrist was and Rendell said he didn't know – and, surprise, surprise, Hoffmann hadn't bothered to update me about this.

I arranged a meeting with Jack Farrow but he was so busy with his existing caseload, I had to wait until October: in the meantime, I sent him lots of information on the case to give him as much background as possible prior to our meeting. I also had to pay his up-front retainer of two thousand, five hundred dollars. Farrow had offices in both Austin and San Antonio, and Pamela, once again very kindly offering me her support during my stay, drove me to the Austin office to meet him.

Once inside the rather smart office suite, I was met by Farrow's two female assistants and was asked to take some psychological tests before I met him. These proved to be nothing like the scale of the testing we had been put through by Rowe, and quite soon I was sitting in Farrow's office, telling him my story. He said he would arrange to meet Joss and Michael, but he wasn't sure just how much he would be able to do, given that I would have to go through the necessary legal proceedings again. I didn't care about that, I just wanted someone to find out what was really wrong with Joss – to unearth exactly what had happened to him.

When I asked Joss who his psychiatrist was, he gave me the name of Lena Baird. I did some searching on the internet, found her contact details and wrote her a letter, explaining who I was and asking very politely if I could speak with her. It came as no big shock when I received nothing back, and all I got from her secretary was to be advised that any patient over the age of sixteen is protected by absolute patient confidentiality.

Returning home again, I waited to hear from Jack Farrow, excited that I had found a psychologist who understood PAS. After a few weeks, I heard from Bob Hoch and the news he gave me was *not* what I had been hoping for. He told me that Jack Farrow had entered into legislation against his two assistants who were now facing criminal charges for, apparently, falsifying the business accounts and stealing from Farrow. It was a massive law suit and it prevented Farrow from undertaking any work on my behalf.

Another hope dashed, another dead end, and another retainer paid out and never refunded. Nothing more ever came of my contact with Jack Farrow.

Chapter thirty-two

alarm bells

Another new year came around, and it was now 2006, exactly seven years since my little boys were taken from me, seven years since my life was turned into this hell on earth. Through it all, and against all odds – mainly those thrown at me by JP – I had fought to keep in touch with Joss and Michael. No matter how hostile they were toward me, no matter how harrowing the experience was. Of course, I would very often cry helplessly after the worst of these occasions, but I knew from my PAS studies that, somehow, in some way, the children would be taking it in that I always made the effort, that I was always there, that I really did care about them, however they may behave toward me.

One day in February, I tried to ring to speak to them and I couldn't get through to the Proctors' number in Texas. I found out, after trying for two weeks, that their phone service had been disconnected, and, in a panic, I wrote to Hoffmann to tell him there was no means of communication for me to contact the boys. I left it a little longer, in case they were reconnected, as I was all too aware of the highly unstable financial affairs in the Proctor household that meant this kind of thing was not unusual.

A month passed and I started to feel seriously alarmed. I had no way of knowing what was going on over there, and we all know it's when you have absolutely no idea about something that your mind goes into overdrive. I knew JP had a sister in Texas and I still had an old address book with her number in it – I frantically dug the book out and couldn't wait to dial her number, praying she would still be there. I was so relieved to hear her voice at the other end, even though we hadn't spoken for about seventeen years. She told me the Proctors were in dire financial straits and were about to be evicted from their home. I said I must have a number somewhere for Tess' parents in Houston and that I would give them a ring to ask for Tess' mobile number.

The panic in her voice shot down the line: *"Oh, no! I wouldn't do that!"*, she gasped the words into the phone and I asked myself why would JP's sister be so concerned about me contacting his wife's family? She repeated the words and I asked her why I shouldn't make the call. She told me JP and Tess hadn't been getting on very well recently.

That was it. I was now determined to ring Tess' parents and I flicked through the old address book, so pleased that I hadn't ever thrown it out. I bet JP would never imagine I would still have these details! I dialled the number straight away. A croaky Texan voice came down the line and I was speaking to Tess' father. I told him about the phone being disconnected and the threat of eviction, but, before I could say any more, the old man said something that really shocked me. *"Tess lives here with us. They've been divorced for over a year."*

Apparently, JP had served Tess with divorce papers in December 2004 and he'd left the family home in Austin and had been living in Houston for the past fifteen months. Tess had stayed on until the end of the school term in May, then she left with her own son and moved in with her parents. He told me she had wanted desperately to take my boys with her, but JP wouldn't let her.

My mind was racing. Who, then, was looking after my two boys? Oh, my dear God! The Proctor grandparents, aged

248

eighty-five and ninety-seven! The doddering ancient remnants of the couple who created the monster himself were in charge of my incredibly vulnerable children.

Of course, this information had been kept from me intentionally for over fifteen months – bear in mind that I had been speaking to the boys regularly on the phone until a month or so ago.

Then, as Tess' father and I were chatting, Tess' mother, Gladys, took the phone and things became even more intriguing. She told me Tess wasn't allowed to talk to me because she had signed a 'gagging order' as part of the divorce agreement. Well, wasn't that just the sort of game I'd have expected JP to play? But he hadn't reckoned on dear Gladys – she was in *her* house, it was *her* phone and, by golly, she was going to talk to whoever she wanted to! He had no control over her.

I told her what had happened when he divorced me – his ridiculous fictitious drama about being a CIA agent, and so on. *"Oh, my God!"* Gladys exclaimed at hearing this, *"He said exactly the same to Tess!"* Oh, what a surprise. I told Gladys of my grave concerns for the boys and she said Tess wasn't allowed to speak to them either. I said JP's parents were way too old to have charge of two teenage boys, especially boys diagnosed with mental health problems. When we ended our conversation, good old Gladys gave me Joss' and Michael's mobile numbers. I didn't even know they had mobiles.

I called the boys and they were truly surprised to hear from me. I told them I knew all about Tess not being with them, and asked them why they hadn't told me. They said it was none of my business – JP had trained them well, indeed.

Apparently, he was furious when he found out I had contacted his sister and Tess' parents: he threatened Tess again not to speak to me but he had obviously omitted to include Gladys in the gagging order! I admit I was delighted to hear of his rage at my actions – there had been so very little in my favour for so long, I couldn't help but enjoy any tiny victory, however pathetic that may seem.

I tried to call Gladys again but Tess' father answered and said she couldn't speak to me; it was so patently obvious that JP had threatened them all – no doubt telling them that, if they disobeyed, the CIA wouldn't cough up the child support.

Knowing what the boys' situation was, I didn't get any sleep for two nights. The thought of them living with the aged – and uncaring, as I knew for myself – grandparents took this beyond dysfunctional. The question was, what could I do now?

Desperate, I wrote to the ever helpful Hoffmann and told him what I had found out, including the boys' latest move to a Travel Lodge where they had stayed for the past month. They didn't even have a proper home now and this was not acceptable, especially given Joss' state of mental health. I told Hoffmann in my letter that he could check with JP's sister or Tess' parents if he wanted any verification, and I gave him their numbers. He never did.

Hoffmann did suggest that I contact the Texas social services to see if they could help, although he admitted he wasn't at all optimistic. He said they were already overloaded with cases 'far worse than this one', but – to my great surprise – he offered to help me with this. Of course, he never did, so I called the social services office and I described to them the situation the boys were living in. How naïve I was, to even think they would do anything. They asked me if the boys had 'a roof over their heads', to which I replied *"Well, yes, but it's not a proper, stable home – it's a Travel Lodge!"* and they then asked if there was 'food on the table' to which I replied "Well, I suppose, yes, there will be."

In that case, they told me, there was nothing they could do. They said the boys were sixteen years old and so they could choose who they lived with, regardless of the grandparents' ages, Joss' mental health or anything else, for that matter.

One more dead end. How many can there be in one lifetime, I wondered.

Chapter thirty-three

finally, some news

I had tried every avenue I could think of and there was no more I could do to recruit any professional help. My only option now was to keep the telephone contact going and hope that passing time would bring some change. At least the boys began to warm to me a little when we spoke, although they never wanted to chat for long, which made it very difficult. But it was all I had, and it was better than nothing.

The boys now lived with the aged grandparents in Austin, while their doting father lived in Houston and hardly ever saw them. He was constantly travelling away on his 'business fundraising' quests, and I guess by now he had lost interest, plus he was moving on in his own life – yet again – to pastures new. He was to re-marry in 2010 to someone he had met on the internet, a woman twenty years or more his junior, an artist with no children of her own.

The rest of 2006 passed by with no real progress, another new year dawned and 2007 then became the year in which I was to feel boundless gratitude to the world of modern technology, when something extraordinary and wonderful happened.

Thanks to Facebook, Michael had been in contact with his favourite cousin – they were the same age and had always enjoyed a very good relationship. She lived in London and she found out that Michael's favourite band, Muse, were to be performing at a London venue, and she was trying to encourage him to fly over to see the band with her. My niece told me of her plan and I knew the seed had been planted. Of course, I was going to do everything in my power to make this prospect as attractive as possible to Michael, and I offered to pay his air fares. JP was, naturally, absolutely furious at the whole idea and, at first, he said Michael could only stay for three days, to which I replied that was ridiculous. His next attempt to scupper the plan was to tell Michael, who needed a new passport, that the Texan authorities were clamping down tightly on issuing new passports, because there were so many Mexicans jumping the border and the Immigration department had so many problems with this . . . blah, blah. All utter rubbish, as always, but Michael believed it. He did, however, really want to make the trip: he would know he'd be expected to stay with us, which may have given him doubts, but the sway of seeing the band in a live performance and spending time with his cousin eventually won the day. He put JP under a great deal of pressure to let him come over; after all, this was to be a free holiday for Michael, with us paying for everything, so what argument could JP possibly have? He finally had no option but to give in – I had already paid for the flight tickets to help things along and Michael must have felt he was already on the plane!

In true JP fashion, he just couldn't let it happen and back off for even a few days. He had to write me a nasty e-mail, which he tried to make appear 'official', and which he insisted I sign to accept his terms and conditions as detailed in the message, before he would, at last, agree to the trip. The e-mail made my blood boil and my skin crawl at the same time, but I signed it, just to shut him up. The e-mail read:

FINALLY, SOME NEWS

"**Subject**: Michael

Pamela – First, it is my fervent hope that Michael has a good time on this trip and that you and Michael can begin a process of reconciliation. Further, that he get to know his sister and cousins first hand once again. To insure that process I have the following recommendations and requirements:

1. I am really uncomfortable with Michael staying in Edward's and your home. I know you would never hurt him. But, this is Edward's home and Edward is truly entitled to his own castle. I would fully understand him bearing resentment to me and the kids given the whole court process. I do not want Michael in harm's way. Therefore, I have given Michael strict instructions if he feels cornered or if there is excessive drink where emotions may rise or old angers fuelled to leave immediately and go to the nearest other Bed and Breakfast or hotel.

2. Mike is a wonderful boy and I trust his good judgment over how late to stay out. However, under no circumstances do I want him riding with anyone regardless of age who has been drinking.

3. This trip is not about who is wrong or right. The trip is an opportunity for Michael and you to begin to bridge differences. I have not blocked your calls what ever you think and I am not stopping the trip even though I legally have the right to do so until his 18th birthday.

4. Michael has given strict instructions

to reimburse you for the tickets immediately upon his arrival. Further, he will be given cash for expenses or emergency hotel accommodations if necessary.

5. For Michael to go I want your absolute assurances if Michael feels threatened he can leave immediately no questions asked, no attempts to convince him otherwise.

6. Please stop quizzing the kids, my relatives or Tess about my business, my whereabouts or anything else this is frankly none of your business, creates more tension especially with Joss and adversely affects your own goal for reconciliation.

7. I want item 5's assurances in writing so that Michael can carry them with him to show to the authorities if necessary. I apologize if this hurts you but, Mike's safety comes first.

JCP"

"Mike's safety comes first". . . I have no way of describing what I felt on reading those words, let alone the garbage that went before them. This man, this person who had created all of the years of court cases, court orders, therapists, psychologists, psychiatrists, cross-Atlantic flights, hotel bills, mountains of correspondence, massive expense, on top of the heartache, misery and loss, the damage to the children's minds that may never be mended – this evil, loathsome person dares to speak to me in this way. After everything he had done, had caused, he had the audacity to believe he could extend his self-gratifying control into my very home – but, if appearing to play his stupid game and accept his 'rules' would get Michael over here, with us, what the hell?

We waited for several months before Michael actually got his passport, which should have taken two weeks maximum, but, as ever, JP just had to be obstructive at every turn and exert control. He was obviously doing his damnedest to try to wreck the whole thing and was probably hoping Michael would get fed up and change his mind: as it was, the delay meant we had to change the flights, which added to the cost, and Michael ended up missing the Muse concert. Fortunately, by this time he had built up his anticipation of the trip and had set his heart on coming over, so he still made the journey. Michael, my son, was coming to stay for a whole week! I could scarcely believe it.

As I drove to Heathrow to pick him up, I was so excited and nervous, my stomach was churning and I hadn't slept – but I was wide awake. This was such a huge, momentous breakthrough and I just had to make sure it went well, try to make it perfect. I was putting myself under great pressure. Would I even recognise him? I'd only seen him briefly with John Rendell and that was ages ago . . .

A tall, boyish-faced young man came through the Departures doorway, walked over to me and gave me a big hug. Six feet, four inches tall – not quite my little boy any longer! We drove down to Bournemouth and chatted in a rather superficial way, nothing deep and meaningful, as much as I was desperate to talk to him about the years that had passed by, about poor Joss, about the mess his father had made of all of our lives. But I just had to keep myself in check.

We arrived at the house. Michael said hello to Edward and shook his hand, as if everything was normal, but he obviously felt uncomfortable. He retreated to his room a lot while he was with us, just to be on his own; he was still very young to have to handle this – especially after all he had been put through, things an average child wouldn't even dream of – and I knew this was going to take time.

The first night he stayed, I crept up to his room and I just stood and looked at him while he slept. I had missed so much of his life – the last time he was with me he was a child, and now, here was this young man, my son and yet, a stranger. I remembered when he was a baby, a toddler, then a little boy. I had missed all of those years of him growing, laughing, learning, crying, hugging, sharing – all of it. I could have stood there forever, just looking at my child who I had missed so much for so, so long, with so much sadness. I had thought this day would never come.

The situation was obviously very stressful for all of us, and I had a lot of advice from close friends as to how I should handle it. I decided the best thing to do was be as 'nice' as I could, make him as comfortable as possible with us, so that he might want to come back again. If I tried to confront him, ask questions, demand information, I knew that would surely just push him further away. I couldn't afford to take that risk, however frustrating it was, however much of a strain it put me under. There was so much to be discussed, but we all pretended everything was fine. There could be no elephant in the room.

Every now and then, I just had to escape to my room to be alone – which sounds crazy, when all I wanted to do was be with Michael, but the situation was so stressful, I had to keep getting away from it all. Michael would go off to my mother's flat, which was only five minutes away; no doubt this was his own form of escape.

Something that was, however, very pleasantly surprising, was that Michael was very good with the children and he played with them easily and comfortably. They took to him, even though they had no idea who he really was: the great thing about children is that they just accept and don't question. This was terrific and helped things along quite a lot. As for me – I wasn't at all used to teenage boys, as I'd missed out on all of that, but I did see Michael as quite immature, which wasn't surprising, considering his background and everything he'd been forced to experience. He'd lived in isolation, missed school for two years, and spent his teens with the decrepit grandparents. The poor boy had been through so much, and I tried to make allowances for that.

Anyway, somehow, we got through the week unscathed and, to prove it wasn't a total disaster, Michael came back to stay for Christmas that same year. JP actually paid for the flights this time (his promise of the reimbursement for the first flights never materialised, as Michael had turned up absolutely penniless – what would have happened if he *had* wanted to flee from us and go to a hotel? So much for all of those stupid conditions!) and I do think Michael had put pressure on him to put his hand in his pocket, instead of making the poor lad come over again with no money of his own.

Michael had a whale of a time over Christmas, visiting his cousins in London, being taken out for meals and playing with his step-brother and sister – all very nice. He did find meal times a bit much, when we were all sat together at the table, and, during Christmas dinner, he suddenly got up and left the table to go upstairs to his room, saying he didn't feel well. I followed him up and he didn't look too good: he told me he had been sick. I suppose he found the situation of being surrounded by all of us a bit too much to handle.

Michael's next visit was the following summer. Although I realised that the approach we had adopted of not pressing him for any information or any discussion about the past was working, in that he was obviously happy to keep coming back, this was proving too much of a strain for me. I was bursting with feelings I couldn't express and I felt I was pretending all the time, which meant I was constantly on edge. I actually had a panic attack at one point, which had never happened to me before – even with all of the heartache and headaches I'd already lived through.

Michael was enjoying our hospitality, but this was always on JP's terms. He always spoke very highly of his father and grandmother – you can imagine, after everything they had caused me, my children and my family, this was unbearable to have to listen to. Michael's position of having a 'foot in both camps', as it were, was not working; there had simply been way too much water under the many bridges. Our situation wasn't like a normal divorced couple, where the children see both parents – this was an extreme case and JP was still imposing his control over us in whatever ways he could. Michael seemed to be treating his visits to us as if he were staying with an aunt and uncle for a holiday. I felt demeaned, debased, and holding my emotions in all of the time was proving increasingly difficult.

The inevitable happened, and one day I just couldn't take it any longer. I took Michael out for lunch to the local pizzeria and, as soon as we were seated, I just came out with it: *"Have you any idea of the devastation our family has been through because of what happened in the past?"* Immediately, Michael's face was streaming with tears and he just kept repeating *"the guilt . . . the guilt . . . the guilt"*. He started shaking and got up from the table, heading up the stairs towards the cloakrooms. After fifteen minutes, I decided he'd probably left the restaurant and I wished I hadn't said anything. He did eventually come back to the table and I knew I just had to back off; it was obviously too painful to push him to that place. I was dealing with emotions here that I didn't have the skills to cope with; to do this, it would take a professional therapist and I wasn't one. All I could do was back-track to make Michael feel better, so I told him that none of what had happened was his, or Joss' fault. *"You are not to blame, you were only ten years old – just a little boy."* I had to take the guilt away from him.

After a while, Michael became calm again and we changed the subject. I knew he was nowhere near ready to talk in any depth about the past and I must leave well alone until the day dawned when he could handle it. For now, I decided, I had to be content with this 'compromise relationship' – Michael was my son but he was still completely controlled by JP.

Whenever I asked about Joss, Michael was very cagey and it made him uncomfortable. He would just say *"Joss is fine"*, which I knew was rubbish, but Michael was so evasive I knew not to press the subject. JP's control was clearly evident, even from the other side of the world. My plan was to get Michael to come to live with us eventually, and Joss would follow – I could fly out to bring him back. But I wasn't quite there yet: there was more work to be done and I needed time to do it.

Michael did come back again for a couple of weeks in 2009. He had made some friends now, and was very pally with the son of a friend of mine, so he had a proper social life here, going to the pub or a club with friends in Bournemouth.

Chapter thirty-four

the truth will out

Meanwhile, as Michael built a life for himself here, I was constantly checking out the internet to see if there was any information about JP's activities as the con man he had always been. I knew he would still be out there, scamming and ripping off unsuspecting individuals, just like he had been doing for years. It was the only thing he knew how to do, it was what he was used to – and he was, most unfortunately, good at it. And there it was, on my computer screen, just what I had been hoping for – no less than three separate complaints about him being involved in fraud.

This complaint was filed in March 2009 by a young attorney in Houston: *"This site will be used to provide updates on a lawsuit filed against JP and his companies for failure to pay their obligations . . . I have personally lent JP and his companies twenty-five thousand dollars of which not one cent has been returned. I also heard of at least two individuals who have each lent JP funds in excess of three hundred thousand dollars of which not one cent has been returned . . . Perhaps you have had the privilege of hearing the same excuses and lies that I have over the last several years about why funds haven't been returned. My filing suit wasn't a sudden action, it was the result of the frustration of being lied to and promised many different things. JP has failed to return calls and emails which, in my opinion, seem to reflect that he doesn't really care about his creditors. What he does seem to care about though is getting even more funds from other sources."* This was followed by details of the lawsuit's progress, together with comments from JP and his attorneys.

One comment, posted in May 2009, simply warned people to *"Stay away"*, and another, from a doctor who had been approached by JP asking for a cash investment in his business, said: *"This guy is a class con artist. He came to see me in Austin and tried to convince me that there was money to be made by aligning myself with him and his partner [name]. He basically offered me some sweetheart deal with incredible returns for some funds up front. Now why do you need money with all these patented technologies? He gives you a great presentation of all the people he knows, places he's been and companies he's headed. And yet he had nothing on him through a simple Google search. If you know so many people then why are you running out on a lunch bill? He goes by the name of [name], [name], as well as others. He claims to have companies called [name], [name] and others but hey guess what? Our private investigator has determined that none of these exist either."*

Was JP's castle starting to show cracks? Could things finally be starting to turn my way?

Chapter thirty-five

recent events

In 2010, Michael arrived again and this time he stayed for four months altogether. Being aware of the information on the internet about JP's dubious 'business' activities led me to believe that this was the reason for Michael's extended visit; if JP had run out of money again, it made sense for Michael to live with us until such time as more money was found. JP couldn't afford the rent on Michael's apartment in Austin, and Michael had been sleeping on various friends' couches, which can't have been very nice for him; he had cut short the college course he had been taking and was basically drifting.

This trip was different from the previous ones Michael had made. I soon began to sense a definite dissatisfaction with his life in America. He knew absolutely that he didn't want to work with his father: he was still only twenty-one and he hated the prospect of working with much older people. He told me that what he really wanted was to be an actor! I could overhear him arguing heatedly with JP on Skype about the work issue, with Michael insisting he didn't want to join his father's business. He was obviously in a very confused place just now.

It was during this longer stay that I learned so much more about life in the Proctor household. Michael finally began to open up and confide in me; I just kept quiet and listened to everything he was saying. The true facts were a long way from the happy family picture that JP had painted, with them all baking cakes and praying together! Tess, as I and others had suspected, was an alcoholic and was using hard drugs: Michael wasn't certain of everything she took but cocaine was definitely her drug of choice and she took a lot of pills as well, which Michael said her hairdresser supplied. Tess would often send Michael upstairs to fetch the pills for her; he remembered one time when they were staying in a hotel in Albuquerque and the hotel staff had to support her and escort her and the two boys back to their room, because she was so drunk she couldn't stand up. He said she was always complaining about meals when they ate out, always sending food back and making a scene. Apparently, the grandparents hated her, and – lo and behold – so did Joss and Michael. If Michael committed some minor misdemeanour, she would ground him in his room for several days at a time, and she would suddenly turn on him for no reason, which was probably a result of the alcohol and/ or drugs.

I was appalled and incensed to hear first-hand that my children had been existing in this way for so many years. The Proctors had conned the courts, the judges, the psychologists, the therapists (all except one, that is) for all of that time. The boys couldn't have been placed into the hands of anyone more inappropriate, more damaging – how could all of those 'professionals' have got this *so* wrong?

I had kept up with my studies of PAS over the entire thirteen years, and I bought the latest book, which was on the subject of the adults who PAS children become. *Breaking the Ties that Bind*[6] is by Amy Baker and in it she interviews many young adults who had been victims of PAS when they were little children. They explain what life was like in the home of the

---

6   *Breaking the Ties That Bind, Amy J. L. Baker, PhD, published by W. W. Norton & Company, New York and London 2007.*

alienator; each family presented an image of the perfect household, but, behind closed doors, there was often some other form of abuse taking place.

As I read this, I remembered Ryan's suggestion in his report that the accusations the Proctors were slinging at me and Edward could possibly have been projections of things they were actually carrying out. I had to fight hard to stop my mind going too far down this road.

About two months into Michael's long stay in 2010, we got him a job as a waiter in our local indoor sports club, and I sorted him out with a British passport so that he could work here legally. I know the job wasn't great, but it was something to occupy him and earn him a little money; he had nothing to pay for while he lived with us, so there was no pressure to earn more. Plus he could take advantage of the club's facilities, and I provided the taxi to collect him after his shift at around eleven o'clock.

As well as having to hold back my urge to question Michael about the past, to tell him everything from my side of things, I had a very serious issue with never knowing if what I was seeing and hearing was the real Michael – or yet another manifestation of his father's control. Having seen for myself the horror of just how distorted his thinking had been, to the point of giving extremely convincing performances when telling others about the 'abuse' Edward and I were supposed to have inflicted on him and Joss, I had no way of knowing whether Michael was *being Michael* or if he was, indeed, still JP's unwitting puppet.

In November, JP travelled to Ireland 'on business' and Michael flew out from Southampton to Dublin to meet up and stay with him for three days. When I drove to the airport to collect him on his return, he wasn't there and it appeared he had missed his flight. I found out later that, in order to save money, Michael had taken a ferry to Holyhead and from there, a train to London. Oblivious to this change of plan, I was stuck at Southampton airport and so decided my best course of action would be to drive to Wimbledon to stay at my sister's place and have Michael meet me there, then I could drive him back to Dorset the next day.

Michael turned up late and my sister had a bit of a go at him, resulting in the two of them falling out. The following day, I drove him back down to Bournemouth, by which time I was getting very tired and my guard was obviously down. I started talking and it all came pouring out, everything I had been so careful to keep quiet about. I cried and cried, and it was like a floodgate had opened; I think the strain of the past few months, spending time with Michael, taking care of him and making sure he was OK and never being able to really talk to him, was all too much and there just had to be a release. A lot of the stress I felt was undoubtedly caused by never knowing if he had another agenda, always desperately trying to work him out. But my outpouring got me nowhere – Michael didn't even appear to be listening to me.

As we pulled up outside the house, Michael jumped out of the car, saying *"I'm going to Granny's."* He was desperate to escape from the uncomfortable situation and he went straight to the sanctuary of my mother's flat. Inside the house, I paced up and down, still full of what I had wanted to say to him. I was very tired, very tearful and completely frustrated because there was no-one there to talk to. I still had things I needed to say and so I rang my mother and told her I was coming over to her place. As soon as I saw Michael, I carried on – I told him I knew it had all been one big plan that he and Joss had had with JP; I said if he had really been abused, why not tell someone at school, or a friend – anyone. He said, *"I suppose there could have been a better way to do it."* Do what? Move to the States because their father had made them a better offer? I asked him, what about poor Joss, living with a ninety-year-old grandmother, and Michael seemed to think this was perfectly fine.

I told him about the complaints I had found posted on the internet from people accusing his father of stealing vast amounts of money from them by lying about his 'business' activities, but Michael really didn't want to hear this. He was in total denial about everything. I asked him what would happen to Joss when grandmother was no longer around – would he end up in some sort of home? I tried to get him to understand that I was only saying these things because I was concerned for him and Joss, and because I didn't want to see them left in a real mess on the other side of the globe.

It turned out that I was right to suspect ulterior motives, as a plan had been hatched while Michael was with his father in Ireland. It was plain to see he had lost interest in his job at the club, not caring if he turned up late and so on. When Christmas came around, he announced that he was returning to the US for two weeks. He had mentioned this when he first arrived, and I have to say I was a bit surprised because I thought he had had enough of life over there. Anyway, he flew back to the States and said he'd be back with us on the fourth of January.

The fourth of January arrived but Michael did not. There was no word, no e-mail, no phone call – nothing. I was devastated. I felt betrayed and – the best word I can find – wounded. We had done so much to help Michael, to support him, to make him feel comfortable while he was here, and he had double-crossed us. That hurt terribly, and I realised I was feeling almost as bad as when the boys were first taken, twelve years before. Even the timing was the same. To be given a glimpse of what life could be with Michael back, then to have him snatched away again, was torture revisited.

Of course, I tried to get in touch with him, but never got any reply. I e-mailed but nothing came back. Hugo left him a message on Skype without me knowing, begging him to come back, telling him *"Michael please come home, Mum really misses you and she's crying all the time."* I left my own message on his answering machine, *"Michael, this is your mother. I hope you feel good. You have betrayed me."*

Months passed by and my feelings didn't subside. I took to comfort eating – it's what I've always done in times of extreme worry or stress.

When JP met Michael in Ireland, he had dangled a carrot that he knew Michael couldn't resist. An apartment in Austin, the university town where his friends lived, where there was so much opportunity for young people, so much life – Michael's favourite place. A much better prospect for a twenty-one-year-old than a waiter's job in a small English market town.

After several months of being swamped by all the wrong feelings, I started to think a little more clearly again. I knew JP was always full of promises that never materialised, and so it was just a matter of time. I had learned to forgive Michael for not keeping in contact, and I truly believed in the value of 'keeping the door open', so that, whenever things went wrong again for him – as they no doubt would – he knew he could count on me.

Chapter thirty-six

two young men – Michael

Over time, the feelings of overwhelming disappointment, anger at the cruel betrayal, and the pain of loss all diminished as I was able to put things into some sort of perspective. Michael was still very young – emotionally younger than his years – and was obviously still very much in the grip of his father's powerful influence. I couldn't keep on being hurt and angry at Michael, so, again, I gave him the benefit of the doubt and decided I had to wait and see what transpired. I knew JP was behind everything that had happened and I knew equally that he would let Michael down again. Then, where would Michael be able to turn? I had to let him know that there was always a safe place for him with me: he was my son and, no matter what he had or hadn't done, I couldn't turn my back on him.

Once Michael knew I was no longer going to be 'off' with him, we managed to regain some contact and we spoke on the phone now and again throughout the year. Michael started working as a runner for a senator in Austin – not a well-paid job, but he was being heavily subsidised by JP, including the apartment he was living in. Michael couldn't care less where the money was coming from, as long as he was in the place he loved, among his friends, enjoying the 'bright lights, big city' lifestyle. I knew it was all a trick, just to get him away from me again. I knew it, but Michael didn't.

I was dead right and what happened in July 2011 showed JP up for the spineless coward he truly was. Michael received an e-mail from JP's 'business colleague' informing him that he could no longer be subsidised and that he had to go and work with his father. This had, of course, been JP's game plan all along, to get his own son to help him in his scamming and deception to take money from people who believed they were buying shares in a successful business – who better to mould for this position than your own flesh and blood, someone you had been controlling for most of his life? And JP didn't even have the guts to tell Michael himself, but gave that unpleasant task to his colleague.

Michael then had no choice but to move in with JP (who was hardly ever there), Joss and granny, in JP's new wife's house in Harpers Ferry, West Virginia. They lived in a tiny village in the middle of nowhere, with a population of three hundred! This was not a place a young man would choose, and I knew Michael hated being there. The New Mrs Proctor, Jodi, made it clear that she didn't like the boys – she was afraid of Joss and didn't want to be anywhere near either of them. Apparently, whenever she was home from her teaching travels, the boys had to stay in a hotel. It was a very odd set-up all round. As for Michael's 'job' with his father, that was all very strange, too. There was no office or base of any kind to work from, and Michael was expected to follow JP around on his travels, trying to 'raise funds' for his various companies. I found out later that Michael wasn't even being paid! He only received expenses.

After about four months of life in Harpers Ferry, Michael was totally fed up with everything and was on Skype, asking me if he could come over to England. He must have been really desperate to be able to ask, after what had gone before, and he pressured JP into buying him an airline ticket (I think this was paid for with Air Miles). So, within twelve months of Michael walking out of my home, he was back on the doorstep.

When I picked him up from the airport this time, the feeling of being 'used' came flooding back and I just had to be a bit more straight with him. I told him I hadn't forgotten what he did last year, how he had left without letting me know what was happening. I made it clear to him that he had hurt my feelings badly.

Then Michael told me he was meeting his father in London at the coming weekend, after which they would fly to Ireland and then return to the States. He said he would come back to England in May! All rubbish, I knew from experience, and it made me angry to have to listen to these ridiculous plans of JP's that would never materialise, but all of which Michael believed, every time. JP's influence on Michael was so apparent, so strong, I could almost feel his presence in my own home, and that made me seethe inside. I asked Michael if he was just using my home as a pit-stop in between his father's crazy business arrangements. I hated the feeling that my son could just use me like that.

And so it turned out, JP didn't come to London that weekend, nor any other weekend for that matter. He never came at all, which pleased me because I thought, maybe now Michael will start to see what the reality was, that JP's plans always fell through, and maybe realise that he needed to extricate himself from his father's crazy world where he was going nowhere fast.

The first two days of Michael's stay brought great revelations: he opened up as never before and it just all poured out. He hated life in Harpers Ferry and he hated the 'job' with JP and the 'colleague'. No pay, mixing with people in their fifties and sixties, his father buying him expensive suits that no-one ever got to see . . . This was no real life for a twenty-two-year-old and Michael was well and truly miserable.

More interesting by far, Michael opened up about his father – the man he had hero-worshipped for all those years: the cracks were really starting to show now, and they were far bigger cracks than before. Michael described JP as 'paranoid and greedy'. They had been on enough business trips together for Michael to observe for himself how JP would turn down many very reasonable offers for shares in his companies, because he was terrified to relinquish even a minor part of the business in case that buyer could eventually take over completely! Michael said he had witnessed what these offers were, and we were talking many hundreds of thousands of dollars – even, on one occasion at least, into millions! JP simply could not handle losing any scrap of control. This explains why they constantly ended up with no money, time after time.

This paranoia, Michael said, showed up in all sorts of situations, even when their sixty-year-old neighbour popped in and JP would say *"What's he doing here? Get him out of here!"* Michael said he would tell JP the chap was just being friendly, neighbourly, as people tend to be in a small community, but that was something of which JP had absolutely no concept – he didn't understand what it meant. When we married, I remember wondering why JP had no friends, neither from the past nor the present, and my son was sitting with me now, all these years later, telling me JP had no friends now. The only people in this man's life were either close family or his 'business colleagues'.

Michael had never seen, nor been told about, Ryan's report suggesting that JP was probably paranoid and that the situation with Joss was a 'shared paranoid delusional disorder', otherwise known as a *folie à deux*, which might otherwise have influenced his thinking, and yet, this twenty-two-year-old had recognised that his own father was paranoid. Remember Rowe's testimony when he stated categorically and with total conviction, that this couldn't be a case of shared paranoid delusional disorder because, for that to exist, there had to be *two people who were both paranoid and delusional*, and, in this case, according to Rowe, there was only Joss.

Michael told me JP wouldn't spend any money on the boys, but he would suddenly do something senseless, such as paying a lobbyist one hundred and fifty thousand dollars. Michael was recognising the financial recklessness and irresponsibility, and he didn't like it: there was no thought for the future, no idea of longer-term consequences. Even at Michael's age, he could see how stupid this was.

With Michael taking me into his confidence to this extent, I believed he had finally seen the light and that he would stay this time. Then he threw me completely a couple of weeks later by saying he was going back to the States. He did say, however, that he wouldn't go back to Harpers Ferry, but would return to Austin. I was totally confused, and felt incredibly let down – how long could this go on, this emotional see-saw?

I could do nothing to stop him if he really wanted to go back, but I did ask him why. He told me his name was still on JP's company and so he had to sort something out: he said he had a plan to try to persuade JP to hand over the business to him so that he could sell off parts of it. He was also due to drive Joss and grandmother from West Virginia to Santa Fe, where they were now going to live. I knew JP would never give him the business and I told him it was madness to think he could make it work. I still knew little about the actual 'business' but I did know that JP had given Michael the company credit card to use while in England – and there was absolutely no credit on it!

I went as far as to tell Michael he was being used, and this must have hit a raw nerve, because Michael suddenly claimed he had a violent headache, fled from the room and shut himself in the bathroom. When he had calmed down, I tried to explain how things appeared to me, to anyone not caught up in the JP 'web' of lies and deceit. I said his father had no concern for Michael's personal development as a young man, and was simply using him to take care of Joss and their grandmother. I explained how it appeared that JP had been grooming Michael to end up working for him, and I warned him that he needed to sever all ties with JP, otherwise he would never be able to move forward. I couldn't be sure if any of my words were really getting through but I had to try to make Michael see sense.

He ended up staying for four months; as usual, JP couldn't afford to pay for his air fare, but eventually he did so. I had to let Michael go, but I did make him promise that, if things didn't work out, he would come back, and I tried to reassure him that, if he made the commitment to stay with us, I would then get Joss over here as well. Michael at least agreed to return if things went wrong.

He hadn't been in West Virginia for very long when grandmother, now aged ninety-one, fell down the stairs and banged her head: although she seemed to be OK afterwards, this must have had an effect on her at that age. Michael did drive her and Joss to Austin and then on to Santa Fe – apparently, that's where she wanted to live. Michael certainly did *not* want to, and he had terrible arguments with his father about what he was supposed to be doing. The first time I spoke to him on the phone, he was adamant that he needed to become financially independent of JP, even if that meant waiting on tables. I was extremely encouraged to hear this, as it seemed Michael was really starting to engineer the break from JP's control.

Our second conversation was even more positive: they had been in Santa Fe for five days, staying in a one-star hotel, where they were going to have to remain for five weeks while grandmother sorted the lease on the apartment she wanted. Michael was so stressed, so utterly fed up, he said he felt as if he was heading for a breakdown – he told me how they had all fallen out, and grandmother, as always holding the purse-strings, was refusing to give Michael any money. He said he hated *'these selfish people'* and that he was going to drive back to Austin the following day. My heart leapt with joy – he was finally finding the courage to break away.

We spoke again a few days later and I could hear the stress in his voice; he was going to rent an apartment in Austin and start working as a waiter. I understood him wanting to be there, but he wasn't thinking it through. Sure enough, renting the apartment was delayed, probably due to finances and JP continuing to string him along. The latest plan for Joss and grandmother was that they were due to live together in north Austin and, as for JP, he was going to live in Utah where his business was located.

As always, things appeared disorganised, disparate and – for my sons, truly dreadful.

Joss

Joss' psychiatrist, Lena Baird, referred him to a Dr Erica Silversmith – again, this was someone of whom I had no knowledge, nor had I been given any information, so I looked her up on the internet and found a contact address. On the sixth of February, 2008, I wrote to her, making my feelings clear: *"I am writing to you because I am seriously concerned about his mental well-being and safety."*

I asked her if she was aware of Joss' home environment: he was living with his grandparents who were far too old to be his carers; Joss couldn't make decisions for himself, he couldn't drive, couldn't hold down any kind of job and was very dependent on other people for his day-to-day needs. I told her that, for the past month, Joss had lived in a hotel room with his father – who travelled away for most of the time – and on every occasion when I had called him he had been left on his own and was playing computer games, alone and unattended.

I asked Dr Silversmith how she envisaged Joss' future and I stressed that Joss should not be living with such an unstable lifestyle, given his vulnerable mental state. I also pointed out that she was my only contact outside Joss' immediate family and, as always, it was impossible to have a serious conversation with them about Joss.

I closed by trying to get her to see the danger of Joss' situation. "*. . . Are we all going to sit back and wait for a crisis to happen? It will only be a matter of time or can somebody take action? . . . I appreciate patient confidentiality agreements for patients over the age of 16 but I see this as exceptional circumstances . . .*" and I gave her all of my contact details, asking her to please get in touch with me.

I copied this letter to Hoffmann, who – surprisingly – did get back to me. His letter was short and didn't offer any real help, but at least he wrote it.

"*. . . I am not sure I can offer you many suggestions regarding Joss. Because he is over the age of 18 years old, the court in New Mexico no longer has any authority over him. Since Joss is considered to be an adult under the laws of all states in the United States, the only thing you might be able to do is to petition the appropriate court in Texas where he resides to appoint you as his guardian. You would have to show that Joss is unable to manage his own affairs and you should be appointed as his guardian to make decisions on his behalf, i.e. where he lives, what type of treatment he needs, etc. I am not sure whether this is a realistic option for you.*"

He added that he would be willing to discuss the matter with me, and he supplied his telephone number and e-mail address.

This was the first time, in all of my dealings with him, that he actually provided me with an e-mail address.

I never received any reply, nor even an acknowledgement, from Dr Silversmith. On the fifth of May I wrote again, referring to the previous letter and repeating my serious concerns for Joss.

"When I visited the US in 2004 – the therapist in Austin told me that Joss was being treated for Major Depression with Psychotic Features and was on the appropriate medication for this. He informed me that Joss needed a great amount of stability in his home life and certainly should not be left on his own for long periods of time."

I suggested that perhaps Dr Silversmith had been misled concerning Joss' domestic set-up, explaining that JP was largely absent and that the grandparents were far too old to cope. I ended with: *". . . I am sending out loud warning signals as to what is going on. Please do not let this become a case of pluralistic ignorance before some crisis happens and it's all too late. How much more does the situation need to deteriorate before somebody takes action? I might also add that I can fly out at a moment's notice if you should wish to meet me."*

Again, there was no reply.

This was to be my final attempt to get help from any of the professionals involved. It was clear to me that I was wasting my time and energy on my campaign – however much I might believe in it. I knew the only thing I could do now was to sit tight and play the waiting game, keep the lines of communication open as much as possible with the boys, keep my hopes up, and pray for something good to happen.

Chapter thirty-seven

the here and now

You can't explain to people – even those you know well – what it's like to wait, to hope, to pray, to build your hopes up at the slightest encouragement and then watch those hopes crash and be destroyed, time and time again.

To ache, to hurt, to scream silently inside, to cry so much the tears don't come any more, to spend so many nights without sleep that you feel you must surely die of exhaustion.

To count seconds, minutes, hours that go by so slowly it's as if time simply can't make the effort any longer and has slipped away.

But the most inexplicable part of this horror is the emptiness, the longing, the desperate aching in every part of you – body, mind, soul. Not one tiny cell can escape the pain.

Experiencing heartache for a month, a week, even one single day is bad and I would *never* try to make light of anyone else's suffering. But thirteen years is – well, it's a hell of a long time.

It's a long time of hell.

I think of my boys all the time. Michael is working – a menial job in a kitchen that is both physically tiring and boring – and he is trying to care for his brother, Joss, who is still just the same, dependent on his medication, dependent on Michael, playing computer games and not really living any sort of life. They live in Michael's small apartment in Austin. Michael has admitted to me that he isn't really managing with Joss, and Joss can't be left on his own.

Things came to blows recently when the two had a physical fight, resulting in Joss having to go and stay at grandmother's for a few days. Michael knows granny is not going to be around for much longer – he even has to run errands for her now, get her shopping and so on. Not much of a life for a young man.

He was going to try to get Joss to come with him to stay with us for Christmas 2012, but that didn't happen. I no longer allow disappointment to tear me to pieces. Joss didn't want to come and I can't blame him. Thanks to his father, he believes his mental illness is due to my negligence in 1991 when he had the febrile seizure; he was told I failed to take him to hospital and it was his father who had to come and rescue him. JP also told him I left the marriage, not him, and that I forced him to sign papers so that I could take the boys back to the UK with me.

All lies, but in Joss' fragile mind, probably reality.

As for JP, I heard from Michael that he had been involved in a major lawsuit (no surprise for me) in Nevada and, for about two months, it looked as if he would go to prison. I don't know the full story – I think I've had enough of JP's stories for one lifetime – but, somehow, he managed to worm his way out of it (again, no surprise). And, true to form once more, marriage number five has come to a timely end in divorce.

Apparently, he is planning to move to Ireland. How unfortunate for Ireland.

I have found some more very interesting material on the internet, posted by people who have been persuaded to 'do business' with JP, people who have been conned very badly, and who are warning others to avoid falling into the same trap.

Posted early in 2013, exactly as it appears on the web site, but with the product names, company names, individuals' names and any date/identification detail all changed:

"John Proctor, [name of company withheld]
Complaint 2005333
Date Occurred: XX/XX/2013
Reported Damages: $2,500,000.00
Location: Texas Asks to invest in his biotechnology products then spends all of the money on his personal lifestyle. Sells products for bioremediation etc. [name of product withheld] was the old product name. He now has a new scam called [name of company withheld]
Anonymous Posted XX/XX/2013
We are currently investigating the following individuals: John V. Proctor, Simon H., Andrew H. and other team members mentioned on the [name of company withheld]. com 'TEAM'.

John C. Proctor aka John V. Proctor seems to have been running scams with the following companies based on online reports:"

And there follows a list of different company names, and then a list of further companies which have all been "dissolved under his name".

This message then lists some web sites where information can be found.

"John Proctor stands approximately 6" tall and has dark black graying hair. John V. Proctor has a partner in his crimes by the name of Simon H. from San Diego, California (Carlsbad/Oceanside Area). He is believed to be in the area presently. Simon H. is in his early 50s with sandy blond hair and stands approximately 5"7" – 5"9" in height.

It is currently unknown if all the team members mentioned on this web site are actually aware of their names being used to promote a seeming scam.

If you have any information to add to this investigation, please post here or contact us at [*telephone number provided*]."

So, the game remains the same but the sums of money have really increased. Surely he can't keep getting away with all of this? And no wonder he's planning to move to the other side of the globe!

Michael told me something that really made me smile. He said JP was convinced the world would end in 2012. This was nothing to do with the Mayan calendar or other historical prophecies, but something quite bizarre to do with radio waves. When JP took Michael to meet 'business clients', Michael said JP would bring this into the conversation and he'd tell everyone about his theory. Michael hated this and was terribly embarrassed – he said he was going to have to speak to JP and tell him to keep his mouth shut because people didn't want to hear such rubbish. He had actually reduced one lady to tears because it upset her so much.

Maybe all the years of evil scheming and causing pain to those around him are finally taking their toll. Who knows?

I continue to feel immensely grateful, more so than I can put into words, to those people who took the trouble to look further than the apparent facts of this case, and who believed that I was not guilty of any wrongdoing. I am certain beyond doubt that it was only through their efforts and support that I have emerged from the mental-emotional chaos of the last thirteen years with my mind intact, and for this I will always owe my personal debt of gratitude.

I also thank those professionals whose books I consumed

in my search for knowledge of PAS and everything around it. All of this information gave me strength and validation, and the determination to carry on.

One particular book gave me insight, as I have mentioned, into a world I had never previously recognised, a world of people unlike anyone I had ever known – until I met JP. That book was *Without Conscience*[7] by Robert D. Hare, PhD, one of the books I read while staying at the Rachel Foundation.

I learned that psychopaths, the subject of the book, can *".... successfully cheat, bilk, defraud, con and manipulate people and have not the slightest compunction about doing so. They are often forthright in describing themselves as con men, hustlers or fraud artists."*

"The capacity to con friend and foe alike makes it a simple matter for psychopaths to perpetrate fraud, embezzlement and impersonation, to promote phony stocks and worthless property, and to carry out swindles of all sorts, large and small."

"Millions of men, women and children daily suffer terror, anxiety, pain and humiliation at the hands of the psychopaths in our lives. Tragically, these victims cannot get other people to understand what they are going through. Psychopaths are very good at putting on a good impression when it suits them, and they often paint their victims as the real culprits."

One thing that is apparent in all of the recorded depositions and testimonies throughout the various court hearings, is that JP is not particularly skilled with language – he often used an incorrect word or phrase, but didn't ever seem to realise his error. Hare says *".... psychopaths ... are not necessarily skilled wordsmiths. It is primarily the 'show', not eloquent use of language, that attracts our attention and cons us ... A ... fast-talking psychopath and a victim who has 'weak spots' is a devastating combination. If the psychopath's 'show' is not enough, the adroit use*

---

7   *Without Conscience, Robert D. Hare, PhD, published by The Guildford Press, New York and London 1999.*

of 'stage props' – phony credentials, flashy car, expensive clothes, a sympathy-inducing role and so forth – will usually complete the job."

"Of course, pathological lying and manipulation are not restricted to psychopaths. What makes a psychopath different from all others is the remarkable ease with which they lie, the pervasiveness of their deception and the callousness with which they carry it out."

I was reminded of something else that had really made me so angry in the court hearings and interviews, and that was listening to JP lying and contradicting himself so blatantly, and yet no-one took any notice – no-one thought to examine any further. Hare points this out: *"But there is something else about the speech of psychopaths that is equally puzzling: their frequent use of contradictory and logically inconsistent statements that usually escape detection."*

Hare offers an explanation as to how these people can 'use' others to their own ends, without any guilt or remorse. *"Psychopaths view people as little more than objects to be used for their own gratification . . . Psychopaths, however, display a **general** lack of empathy. They are indifferent to the rights and suffering of family members and strangers alike. If they do maintain ties with their spouses or children it is only because they see their family members as possessions . . . parasitically bleeding other people of their possessions, savings, and dignity; aggressively doing and taking what they want; shamefully neglecting the physical and emotional welfare of their families . . . and so forth."* How many times had I asked myself the question, how can he be doing all of this, causing all of this damage and pain, to his own children? Perhaps now I knew. *"The indifference to the welfare of children . . . is a common theme in our files of psychopaths. Psychopaths see children as an inconvenience."*

For me, possibly, the most interesting part of Hare's book was *"A particularly revealing illustration of the psychopath's ability to manipulate experienced psychiatrists and psychologists*

. . ."and he quotes from a book written about a psychopathic mass murderer: *"Psychiatrists appointed by the court determined that* [he] *was incompetent to stand trial but the psychiatrists at the hospital considered him competent to stand trial. And so it went, back and forth. After a seemingly endless series of contradictory psychiatric evaluations,* [he] *tired of the game and turned his talents to outmanoeuvring the lawyers and the courts."*

As Hare said, I should not jump to any conclusions, but I have the right to my own opinion.

June 2013 . . .

Another summer, although the weather doesn't seem to realise it. I've been hoping for some news from my son, Michael – hoping to hear that he and his brother, Joss, can no longer continue their life in the States, and that they want to come home at last. Michael's most recent telephone calls have led me to believe this could happen any time now.

This news, as yet, has not arrived, and so my book has no happy-ever-after ending. I may yet receive that call, or maybe not. I did contact the authorities in the States to report Joss' situation but they just led me down so many dead ends, I realised I wasn't going to achieve anything.

Michael is still living in his tiny apartment and now has a girlfriend; he has sent me photos of them and they look happy together, a stunning young couple. Michael has turned into a very handsome young man and does not outwardly show the scars of the life he has had to endure.

Things eventually came to a head between the boys and Michael could no longer cope with Joss living at his place, which meant Joss had no option but to go with his father. Joss' days pass in his medication-controlled world, living in one hotel room after another, always on the move. According to Michael, he is left alone for most of the time, no doubt still playing his computer games, denied human contact. I cannot imagine a less happy existence for my poor, sad Joss.

Their grandmother has moved to Tennessee with her ninety-three-year-old sister because they have been allowed to stay in someone's house free of rent. This move is causing problems with Joss being able to collect his disability allowance, because grandmother is listed as his carer and is supposed to go with him to collect the payments along with the money for his medication.

Both boys are waiting for their father to come up with some cash: he owes Michael three thousand dollars – money Michael has earned by hard graft on minimum wages. This made me remember something in Hare's book on psychopaths, where he said that children were just an inconvenience to such people and were there to exploit along with everyone else.

It all sounds so desperate, so tenuous. How can JP possibly keep getting money from people when there is now so much about him and his crimes on the internet? I just wonder how much worse things will get before this situation simply has to change . . .

For my part, I am grateful for the small steps we have been able to take. Michael has been over to visit several times now, and I am in touch with both of them on Skype and on the phone. And they do call me 'mum' now, and not 'Pam'.

Even if they do come home now, even if we could get together and start to build a new, happy life for all of us, I have still lost my two children and will never have them back. They are not children now, they are young men. They don't need a mother to hold them, to protect them . . . all of those things a mother does.

All I can do is keep loving them and keep hoping.

Many people think that child abduction is something that happens in countries where the laws are different from ours, but the increase in unmarried parenting, the increase in marriages between people of different nations and the increase in divorce – all have contributed to a vast increase in the numbers of children being taken from the parent who has custody. Whether the abducting parent believes they are doing the right thing or not, there must be laws which are substantial and which are recognised on both sides, in order for the situation to be resolved.

The International Hague Convention on the Civil Aspects of International Abduction (1980) was formulated to ensure *"the protection of children from the harmful effects of their wrongful removal or retention".* But this does not work. As Catherine Meyer wrote, *"The purpose of the Hague Convention was to provide a simple and straightforward procedure. In this, it has largely failed. Different national approaches to implementing the Hague Convention, the slowness of procedures, the lack of legal aid in some countries, and the excessive recourse to the loophole clause, has meant that most cases of international child abduction remain unresolved. Some children are never located. Others are not returned to their country of origin."*

The laws are inadequate and they must be changed. The longer this remains the law, the more children are at risk, and the more children fall victim to the terrible fate created by parental alienation.

8213867R00160

Printed in Great Britain
by Amazon.co.uk, Ltd.,
Marston Gate.